A Good Beginning for Babies

Guidelines for Group Care

A Good Beginning for Babies

Guidelines for Group Care

Anne Willis and Henry Ricciuti

with

Lynda Deprez, Frances Doney, Deborah Gilman,
Mildred Lovett, and Beverly Meek

National Association for the Education of Young Children
Washington, D.C.

The information in this book was developed in the Cornell University Research Program in Early Development and Education, Department of Human Development and Family Studies, New York State College of Human Ecology, Cornell University, Ithaca, New York.

Preparation of this book, and the research and development program upon which it is based, were supported in part by the National Institute of Education, U.S. Department of Health, Education, and Welfare (Contract NE-C-00-3-0103); and by CEMREL, Inc., a private nonprofit corporation, through funds from the U.S. Office of Education and the National Institute of Education.

A publication of the National Association for the Education of Young Children, 1834 Connecticut Avenue, N. W., Washington, D. C. 20009.

Photographs by Joan Johnston.

ISBN Number 0-912674-43-1.

Library of Congress Catalog Number 74-25867.

Printed in the United States of America, 1975.

Acknowledgements

The information contained in this book comes out of experience over a three-year period in operating a day care program for babies. Much of the credit for these guidelines goes to the caregivers in our program—Lynda Deprez, Frances Doney, Deborah Gilman, Mildred Lovett, and Beverly Meek. Each of them in her own unique style cared for babies with wisdom, sensitivity, and joy. Put very simply, they lived with babies in the manner described in the following chapters. In addition, they were able to be analytical about what they were doing as caregivers without compromising the quality—the spontaneity and creativity—of their interactions with the babies. Their help in developing this book was invaluable.

Appreciation is also expressed to the babies and their families, who seemed to understand exactly that our job was to explore issues related to infant day care. They were very resourceful in exposing us to a wide variety of joys and problems and concerns that would make us wiser in producing these guidelines.

Eliza Lenneberg and Mary Miller's proficiency as typists and their willingness to assume extra tasks made what could have been a tense period of major and minor crises into a surprisingly smooth, easy process. We are grateful for their assistance.

Finally, we wish to thank Helen Bayer, Jennifer Birckmayer, and Robert Bookman, whose careful critical reading of an early draft of the book led to many helpful suggestions. Their thoroughness and perceptiveness are greatly appreciated.

Anne Willis
Henry Ricciuti

Table of Contents

Introduction

This book presents the results of efforts over several years to conceptualize more systematically and make more explicit the essential features of a *quality group care* environment for infants in the first year of life, in the form of a statement of principles, guidelines, and procedural suggestions. The book is intended to be of practical assistance primarily to those people most directly concerned with establishing and maintaining developmentally facilitating group care environments for infants under twelve to fifteen months of age, either in center- or family-based day care settings.

Our overall approach in formulating this statement of principles and guidelines was to develop and maintain a quality group care environment in our own small experimental nursery, and to test and refine these guidelines in the context of our own experience in operating a program. For three years, our infant nursery provided all-day or half-day care on a daily basis for eight to twelve infants who were first enrolled at approximately two to five months of age and remained in the program for about a year. Operation of this infant day care program permitted us to carry on a variety of systematic observations of infants and the nursery environment, to make modifications of caregiving practices, and to study changes in infant behavior which are necessary to provide an experiential basis for elaboration and refinement of the principles and guidelines.

Social pressures and demands for day care facilities and other programs for fostering the development of toddlers and even very young infants who need group care outside the home are very likely to continue to increase during the next few years. There is consequently great need for further information concerning modifications of experience and early development, and for procedural and programmatic guidelines for use by those people concerned with establishing such programs. Some of these guidelines are concerned primarily with such practical issues as health, safety, nutrition, spatial arrangements, and various types of "obligatory" care such as feeding, diapering, and sleeping. Other guidelines deal more specifically with procedures for ensuring that the infant's day-to-day experiences in the group care situation are supportive of normal or healthy development, and perhaps even of optimal development.

During the past few years, there has been an increasing number of theoretically oriented discussions dealing with the problem of specifying the essential nature and major ingredients of developmentally facilitating early childhood environments, with par-

ticular reference to implications for the issue of group care.[1]* At the same time, a number of manuals and other publications have become available, dealing both with important substantive issues and with principles of good care, addressed primarily to those people involved in developing expanded day care facilities for young children.[2]

For the most part, general efforts of the sort just mentioned have tended to emphasize environments and programs for toddlers and preschool children, until very recently, when several manuals concerned with group care of infants in the first year of life have appeared.[3] This emphasis reflects the fact that in the field in general, development of day care programs for infants is a movement of relatively recent origin, so that our experience with such programs is much more limited. It is precisely because experience in developing infant day care programs is so limited, at a time when the social demand for such programs is rapidly increasing, that there is a need for further work to specify the nature of developmentally facilitating group care environments for infants, and for further development of explicit guidelines and principles for creating and maintaining such environments. This, then, was one of the

---

*Footnotes for Introduction are located at the end of this chapter on pages xvii—xix.

central areas of concern of our research and development program.

Until the past six years or so, our society has shown considerable reluctance to provide group day care for infants and toddlers outside their own homes for substantial periods of time. This reluctance was based in large part upon concerns about possible adverse effects of substantial day care experience this early in life, concerns which stemmed largely from some of the early studies of institutionalization and deprivation.[4] Thus, when experimental day care programs for infants and toddlers from low income families began to be developed in the mid-sixties, some of the first evaluative studies focussed on the reporting of data showing that day care in a quality program need not result in a gradual decline in general developmental status or intellectual functioning, as some had feared. In fact, there is growing evidence suggesting that such experience can help prevent the developmental decline which might otherwise have occurred.[5]

While it seems clear that a good group care environment need not have a detrimental influence on infants' and toddlers' psychomotor, intellectual, and language development, and indeed might even facilitate such development, there is great need for continued studies of the possible effects of substantial experience in group care settings outside the home upon the infant's social development, with particular reference to patterns of social attachment within the family and with other significant people, such as caregivers in a group program.[6] This general issue was a secondary area of concern in our research and demonstration program.[7]

Returning to the issue of program development, the problem of specifying the essential features or elements of a group care environment for infants can be approached in a variety of ways. One can, for example, view the problem essentially as that of designing an *infant curriculum*, in the context of a broader concern with providing better *infant education* for very young children generally, whether in group care or in their own homes.[8] This approach tends to focus on the development of a variety of quite specific types of materials and activities which caregivers, parents, or infant educators can undertake with infants on a one-to-one basis, in the interest of fostering the development of particular behaviors, skills, or competencies. The *infant curriculum* approach frequently involves fairly specific instructions for ensuring that all infants in a particular program are regularly exposed to appropriate educational activities for designated periods of time.

A good many of the suggested materials and activities for caregivers and infants growing out of this approach are very useful, particularly in the training of new caregivers. However, our concern with the *infant curriculum*, or *infant education* approach is that it often tends to view the infant's learning environment in very narrow terms, focussing primarily on the specification of various circumscribed activities, with relatively little consideration of the nature of the infant's total experience in a group care setting. **Our own view is that the infant's "curriculum" (a term we prefer to avoid) essentially represents the total experience provided by the particular day care or home setting under consideration.** Opportunities for developmentally facilitating experiences of many sorts are continuously present in the natural course of events in any ongoing infant group care program, both in such obligatory care routines as feeding, diapering, and the management of distress or sleeping, as well as in play periods. Our major approach, then, is to try to make explicit for caregivers a set of guiding principles concerning infant care, with many concrete illustrations, so that the program (or curriculum) is determined by these principles, and is describable in terms of the specific practices and procedures for care which are generated by the principles. We believe that this approach should, in the long run, make it feasible for care-

givers to use the variety of natural opportunities available to them to ensure that the infant's social and learning experiences in the group care setting are indeed supportive of good development, and perhaps even facilitative of optimal development. Moreover, this orientation makes it possible to incorporate within a program various activities as specified in the curriculum approach, but in the context of a broader concern with the appropriateness of each infant's overall experience, given the infant's particular characteristics and patterns of development.

The ideas in this book come out of experience primarily with normal, healthy babies from middle income families, whose parents in most cases were free of the stresses of poverty or other conditions that sometimes make it difficult for parents to care optimally for their children. The babies in the program were developing normally, free of any major physical or mental handicaps.[9] Also, **while our primary emphasis has been on principles for group care of infants in center-based settings, we believe that they provide equally sound guidance for family-based day care or home care.** Appropriate adaptations of the guidelines would be necessary, but they outline quality care in any setting.

In the chapters that follow, we first formulate a general statement of goals and principles of group care for infants, with sufficient elaboration, hopefully, to make the principles meaningful and explicit (Chapter 1). Then we discuss the importance of maintaining a close relationship between group care programs and the families they serve (Chapter 2). These two chapters provide a guiding framework for the remaining sections of the book dealing with various specific aspects of operating and maintaining a quality group care program. It is in the context of these later sections that the principles and guidelines are further articulated and concretized.

Attention is directed first to the overall organization of the program and staffing arrangements (Chapter 3). We then turn to more detailed considerations of program content and operation, organized primarily in terms of the major responsibilities and concerns of the caregivers in the daily operation of an infant nursery. This discussion begins with a brief overview of a typical day in the nursery from the perspective of a caregiver (Chapter 4), and then goes on to a systematic consideration of the importance of ensuring that infants have ample opportunities for meaningful play and learning as a natural part of their daily experience, particularly in the context of social interaction (Chapter 5). Two general areas of infant adjustment which can be greatly facilitated by sensitive caregiving are then discussed: first, the management of crying and the relief of distress, particularly in younger infants; and second, the gradual fostering of self-guided and controlled behavior as infants reach the end of the first year (Chapter 6).

Consideration of feeding, diapering, and naptime (Chapter 7) is relatively brief, and stresses the utilization of these situations as opportunities for learning and social interaction between infant and caregiver. Since the implementation of the kinds of caregiving practices discussed so far depends heavily on the quality of the caregiving staff, a fairly detailed discussion of staff composition, training, and morale is presented in Chapter 8.

The next two chapters deal briefly with the functional arrangement of physical facilities (Chapter 9) and necessary guidelines concerning health and safety (Chapter 10). Finally, in the Epilogue we discuss briefly a number of unresolved general issues and questions of importance to those concerned with infant care, particularly within group care settings.

From the foregoing outline of the content of this book, it is obvious that we have devoted major attention to the implementation of principles of good care through a detailed consideration of sensitive caregiving practices likely to facilitate the development of infants' intellectual, social, and motor competencies. There are a number of important problems and issues relating to infant day care programs which we have not approached, or have covered only briefly, because more complete discussions of these issues are available elsewhere. We have not attempted to provide an overview of normal infant development, a matter of particular importance for caregivers. Caregivers must be knowledgeable about infant nutrition, and this topic does not fall within the scope of these guidelines. We have presented only a brief consideration of such matters as health and safety, physical facilities and space planning, and administrative and fiscal management. Suggested sources of information on these topics are indicated in the appropriate chapter notes.

Setting up a day care center involves special concerns in a number of areas beyond the scope of this book, including licensing. Those people responsible for programs must be thoroughly familiar with the federal, state, or local regulations under which they will operate. In addition to references in the notes for each chapter, there are a number of good general sources of information on setting up day care centers and licensing.[10]

The book was written primarily for use by center or program directors, those people in charge of maintaining program quality and training staff. However, most parts of the book will be useful if read and discussed by the entire caregiving staff. Various ways in which this book and other sources of information can be used in training caregivers are suggested in the chapter dealing with staff training (Chapter 8).

Finally, it should be mentioned that some people may perceive our discussions of goals and principles for infant day care in the chapters which follow as representing unrealistically high standards or expectations, given the practical realities and limitations of operating programs in the field. It is our view that these recommended principles and practices are reasonable and attainable. While it is inevitable that compromises must be made under many circumstances, it is imperative that people involved in group care of infants be continuously working toward providing optimal conditions for fostering infant development.

Introduction—Notes

1. Bronfenbrenner, U. "When Is Infant Stimulation Effective?" In *Environmental Influences*, edited by D.C. Glass. New York: Rockefeller Press and Russell Sage Foundation, 1968.

Caldwell, B.M. "What Is the Optimal Learning Environment for the Young Child?" *American Jounral of Orthopsychiatry* 37 (1967):8-21.

Fowler, W. "The Effect of Early Stimulation: The Problem of Focus in Developmental Stimulation." *Merrill-Palmer Quarterly* 15 (1969):159-170.

Yarrow, L.J. "Conceptualizing the Early Environment." In *Early Child Care*, edited by C.A. Chandler, R.S. Lourie, and A.D. Peters. New York: Atherton Press, 1968.

2. Appalachian Regional Commission. *Programs for Infants and Young Children*. Washington, D.C.: Appalachian Regional Commission, 1970.
  Part I: *Education and Day Care*
  Part II: *Nutrition*
  Part III: *Health*
  Part IV: *Equipment and Facilities*
Chandler, C.A.; Lourie, R.S.; and Peters, A.D., eds. *Early Child Care*. New York: Atherton Press, 1968.

Fein, G.G., and Clarke-Stewart, A. *Day Care in Context*. New York: John Wiley & Sons, 1973.

Grotberg, E. H., ed. *Day Care: Resources for Decisions*. Washington, D.C.: Office of Economic Opportunity, 1971.

Office of Child Development, U. S. Department of Health, Education, and Welfare. *Day Care*. Washington, D.C.: U.S. Government Printing Office.
  1. *A Statement of Principles*, 1971 [DHEW Publication No. (OCD) 72-10].
  2. *Serving Infants*, 1971 [DHEW Publication No. (OCD) 72-8].
  3. *Serving Preschool Children*, 1974 [DHEW Publication No. (OCD) 74-1057].
  4. *Serving School Age Children*, 1972 [DHEW Publication No. (OCD) 72-34].
  5. *Staff Training*, 1971 [DHEW Publication No. (OCD) 72-23].
  6. *Health Services*, 1971 [DHEW Publication No. (OCD) 72-4].
  7. *Administration*, 1971 [DHEW Publication No. (OCD) 72-20].
  8. *Serving Children with Special Needs*, 1972 [DHEW Publication No. (OCD) 72-42].

3. Dittmann, L.L., ed. *The Infants We Care For*. Washington, D.C.: National Association for the Education of Young Children, 1973.

Evans, E.B., and Saia, G.E. *Day Care For Infants*. Boston: Beacon Press, 1972.

Honig, A.S., and Lally, R.J. *Infant Caregiving: A Design for Training*. New York: Media Press, 1972.

Huntington, D.S.; Provence, S.; and Parker, R.K. *Day Care 2: Serving Infants*. Washington, D.C.: U.S. Government Printing Office, 1971 [DHEW Publication No. (OCD) 72-8].

Keister, M.E. *"The Good Life" for Infants and Toddlers*. Washington, D.C.: National Association for the Education of Young Children, 1970.

Provence, S. *Guide for the Care of Infants in Groups*. New York: Child Welfare League of America, 1971.

Tronick, E., and Greenfield, P.M. *Infant Curriculum*. New York: Media Projects, 1973.

4. Bowlby, J. *Attachment and Loss*. Vol. 2: *Separation*. London: Hogarth, 1973.

Provence, S., and Lipton, R.C. *Infants in Institutions*. New York: International Universities Press, 1962.

Rutter, M. *Maternal Deprivation Reassessed*. Baltimore: Penguin Books, 1972.

Yarrow, L.J. "Separation from Parents during Early Childhood." In *Review of Child Development Research, Vol. 1*, edited by M.L. Hoffman and L.W. Hoffman. New York: Russell Sage, 1964.

5. Caldwell, B.M. "What Does Research Teach Us about Day Care for Children under Three?" *Children Today* 1 (1972):6-11.

Horowitz, F.D., and Paden, L.Y. "The Effectiveness of Environmental Intervention Programs." In *Review of Child Development Research, Vol. 3: Child Development and Social Policy*, edited by B.M. Caldwell and H.N. Ricciuti. Chicago: University of Chicago Press, 1973.

Starr, H. "Cognitive Development in Infancy: Assessment, Acceleration, and Actualization." *Merrill-Palmer Quarterly* 17 (1971):153-186.

6. The following papers are accounts of recent attempts to examine possible effects of extended day care experience in the first few years of life on patterns of attachment between mother and child.

Blehar, M. P. "Anxious Attachment and Defensive Reactions Associated with Day Care." *Child Development* 45 (1974):683-692.

Caldwell, B.M.; Wright, C.M.; Honig, A.S.; and Tannenbaum, J. "Infant Day Care and Attachment."*American Journal of Orthopsychiatry*, 40 (1970):397-412.

7. Ricciuti, H.N. "Fear and the Development of Social Attachment in the First Year of Life." In *Origins of Human Behavior: Fear*, edited by M. Lewis and L. Rosenblum. New York: John Wiley & Sons, 1974.

Ricciuti, H.N., and Poresky, R.H. "Development of Attachment to Caregivers in an Infant Nursery during the First Year of Life." Paper presented at meetings of the Society for Research in Child Development, March 1973, Philadelphia, Pa.

See Chapter 3, note 1 for brief summary of the two preceding papers.

Willis, A., and Ricciuti, H.N. "Longitudinal Observations of Infants' Daily Arrivals at a Day Care Center." Technical Report, Cornell Research Program in Early Development and Education. Ithaca, New York: Cornell University, January 1974.

8. Fowler, W. "A Developmental Learning Approach to Infant Care in a Group Setting." *Merrill-Palmer Quarterly* 18 (1972): 145-175.

Gordon, I.J. *Baby Learning Through Baby Play*. New York: St. Martin's Press, 1970.

Lally, J.R. "Development of a Day Care Center for Young Children." Progress Report of the Syracuse, N.Y. Children's Center, 1969-70.

Lambie, D.Z., and Weikart, D.B. "Ypsilanti-Carnegie Infant Education Project." In *Disadvantaged Child. Vol. III*, edited by J. Hellmuth. New York: Bruner/Mazel, 1970.

Painter, G. "The Effect of a Structured Tutorial Program on the Cognitive and Language Development of Culturally Disadvantaged Infants. *Merrill-Palmer Quarterly* 15 (1969):279-294.

Painter, G. *Teach Your Baby*. New York: Simon & Schuster, 1971.

Pekarsky, D.; Kagan, J.; and Kearsly, R. *Manual for Infant Development*. No publisher given. Author's address: Dr. Jerome Kagan, Department of Social Relations, Harvard University, Cambridge, Massachusetts 02138.

9. Granato, S., and Krone, E. *Day Care 8: Serving Children with Special Needs*. Washington, D.C.: U.S. Government Printing Office, 1972 [DHEW Publication No. (OCD) 72-42].

While the focus of this manual is not specifically infants but children of all ages, there are in it many implications for program planning for babies with handicaps.

10. On setting up programs, see:

Day Care Council of New York. *So You're Going to Run a Day Care Service*. New York: Day Care Council of New York, 1971.

Evans, E.B.; Shub, B.; and Weinstein, M. *Day Care*. Boston: Beacon Press, 1971.

Keister, M.E. "Practical Considerations in the Operation of a Center for Infants and Toddlers and Their Families." In *The Infants We Care For*, edited by L.L. Dittmann. Washington, D.C.: National Association for the Education of Young Children, 1973.

Ryan Jones Associates, Inc. *How to Operate Your Day Care Program*. Wyomissing, Pa.: Ryan Jones Associates, 1970.

On licensing:

Child Welfare League of America Standards for Day Care Service (revised 1969). Available from Child Welfare League of America, 67 Irving Place, New York, N.Y. 10003.

Conserco, Inc. *Child Care Bulletin no. 4, subject: A Survey of State Day Care Licensing Requirements*. Washington, D.C.: Day Care and Child Development Council of America, 1972.

Department of Health, Education, and Welfare. *The Federal Interagency Day Care Requirements of 1968*. Reprinted by the Day Care and Child Development Council of America, Washington, D. C.

Office of Child Development, U.S. Department of Health, Education, and Welfare. *Guides for Family Day Care Licensing*. Washington, D.C.: Office of Child Development, U.S. Department of Health, Education, and Welfare, 1973.

Chapter 1

Goals and Principles

Any statement of guidelines for group care of infants rests upon some implicit or explicit set of goals with respect to the children and families served. Although the specific needs being met by a particular program may vary widely, the goals of any program with respect to the infants served must be comprehensive—that is, they must include not only a concern with routine care, health, and safety, but also a concern with the young child's total development, including the child's relationship with his or her family. Thus, when we speak of *quality group care*, we refer to a caregiving environment which ensures that the infant's physical and psychological needs are adequately met, that the sense of belonging to a family is not weakened by the group care experience, that the child has opportunities to develop relationships of trust and attachment to a small number of familiar adults responsible for his or her care, and that suitable opportunities are available for spontaneous, pleasureful learning experiences capable of fostering the growth of the infant's developing competencies.

With continued pressures for infant education, and recognition of the crucial importance of the early months of life for establishing the base for later learning, it is important to stress the view that the best group care setting for a baby's

development is one that approximates a good natural home environment. There are some aspects of a good group care situation that are clearly unlike a home—the most obvious being the continual presence of other babies and adults other than parents. However, this assumption of the importance of a homelike environment can provide a helpful general orientation in designing a program and establishing caregiving practices.

The qualities most parents would like to see nurtured in their young child are the same whether the infant spends most of the time at home or in a day care setting. The following list is not intended to provide a detailed description of the "super-toddler," but outlines some important characteristics of the one-and-a-half- to two-year-old child that are influenced by early experiences:[1*]

1. A sense of belonging to the family, primary attachments to parents and other family members.

2. The capacity to trust people, to feel secure when away from home and with people other than family members. Security implies that the child trusts that his or her parents will return after departures,

and trusts the person in whose care he or she has been placed by the parents.

3. Enjoyment of people, both adults and other children; sensitivity to others and the capacity to interact effectively.

4. A curiosity about the world; the ability to take pleasure in learning and exploring; self-confidence that leads to persistence in overcoming obstacles.

5. Autonomy and independence, the ability to think and act with pleasure by oneself.

6. A sense of oneself as an important person who is cared about, who is able to direct his or her own behavior to some extent (for example, in coping with distress or initiating appropriate social behaviors), and who has an effect on the

*Footnotes for this chapter are located on page 8.

social and physical world (mastery).

7. The ability to comprehend language and events, to begin to be able to express oneself in a way that can be understood; the capacity to solve simple problems.

8. An appropriate level of competence in the areas of locomotion and motor coordination.

Attainment of these goals for toddlers is made easier if the care of young babies is guided by appropriate caregiving principles. The following statement of such principles forms the core of what we regard as a good experience for young children.[2] In the rest of the book we will elaborate and further concretize these principles. It is useless to try to order them by their importance, for they are closely interrelated. Each principle must be considered only in the broader context of the whole set of principles, for each is balanced and complemented by the others.

1. Care for babies must be individualized—that is, caregiving practices should be tailored to the characteristics of each baby. Each baby in a group is unique and must be cared for in an appropriately unique way. The orientation of a group program should be to make the program fit the babies, rather than the babies fit the program. The program should foster caregivers' getting to know individual babies, being aware of differences, and responding appropriately to them. The caregiver's orientation must not be based only upon her* understanding of normal infant development, but should take into account the particular characteristics of each individual baby that she is responsible for. While the developmental goals for each baby in a group will be similar, the ways of achieving them will vary depending on particular infants' needs and characteristics.

2. There should be continuity in the people providing care for babies. A small number of different people should be regularly involved in caring for babies if caregivers and infants are to get to know each other. If this is not the case, individualizing care is very difficult or impossible. Moreover, a relationship of trust and attachment can be established only if contact with the same caregiver is frequent and regular, and there is predictability in the caregiving arrangement. A close relationship with a caregiver can help the baby to develop a more general sense of

_____

* For convenience, caregivers will be referred to with feminine pronouns throughout the book. It is hoped and recommended that males be included as caregivers and in other roles in programs whenever possible.

trust in people. Of course, it is usually not possible in a group care setting for the baby to have literally only *one* caregiver, but there should be very few, and changes in caregiving personnel should be kept to a minimum.

3. Infants should be cared for in a warm, affectionate way that lets them know they are special. Pleasurable experiences shared with caregivers over time will foster the development of positive relationships. Each baby should have the opportunity for some time each day to be alone with the caregiver.

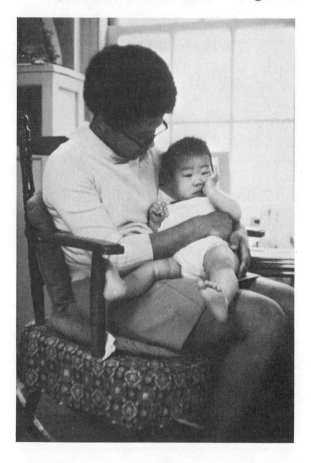

What they do together is not nearly as important as **how** they do it. Treating babies as people who are important, who can bring pleasure to others, helps to develop a positive sense of self. In short, a good caregiver will show respect for the baby as an individual with needs, preferences, and moods. The caregiver will respond appropriately to social overtures and indications of need by the baby and will give the child the opportunity to initiate pleasurable social interactions with her.

4. There should be a balance of consistency or sameness, as well as variety, in both caregiving practices and the physical environment. Consistency alone is neither good nor bad—what is important is consistency in warm, responsive, individualized care. Only if the infant's needs are met in somewhat the same way by the same people each day can the baby learn that the caregiver can be trusted and that the world is a predictable place. Consistency on the caregiver's part must be balanced by sensitivity to changes in the baby and flexibility that allows the adult to change her way of responding to the baby.

Consistency in the physical environment implies that babies learn from sameness as well as from variability. Stability and order in the infant's daily world allow him or her to build up experiences and to make sense out of them. Having

4

the same toys, the same crib, the same basic routines each day gives the infant the opportunity for mastery, for building new competencies on ones already established.

On the other hand, daily experiences should involve new challenges as well as the opportunity to use skills already mastered, for both are important for learning. The environment should offer enough variety to foster exploration and curiosity, to maintain the babies' interest and pleasurable involvement.

5. The social and physical environment in which a baby spends much time should be sufficiently responsive so that the baby learns that he or she can exercise some control over it. If the world is to begin to make sense to the baby, it is important that the baby's actions produce some change in that world. In setting up experiences, caregivers must think about the infants' capabilities and how they can provide the infants with opportunities to have an effect, to do something interesting to the world instead of always being done *to* and *for*. Babies should be cared for in a way that helps them to learn they can have an effect on other people, that overtures on their part will usually lead to predictable responses. Responsivity of caregiving applies to every aspect of care, from providing toys geared to the baby's developmental level and capabilities, to

providing food when the baby signals that he or she is hungry, to responding with a smile and talking to the baby's smiling and talking. The appropriateness of the response is as important as its dependence on the baby's behavior. While the infant's environment should be responsive, it must also be realistic, a place where all behaviors do not necessarily result in predictable outcomes.

6. Every experience is a learning experience, and infants should be cared for in a way that optimizes opportunities for learning and social interaction in daily routine activities. Babies learn attitudes and feelings about people as well as facts about the world and ways of solving problems from the way they are cared for. In short, both social and cognitive learning skills can come out of daily routines where the baby is encouraged to initiate interactions as well as to be responsive to people and things in the environment.

This principle is at the core of the approach in this book, in that the *curriculum* is viewed not as something that happens only **between** feeding, diapering, and naptimes, but **during** them as well. A good program orients caregivers to capitalize on the natural environment and play of the infants. Since routine activities occupy a large part of the infant's day, caregivers should see them not as chores to be done as quickly as possible, but as a time for being together, talking, learning. Also, babies can gain experience very early in life in inhibiting and controlling their own behavior appropriately in the course of these daily activities.

7. Infants need protection from overstimulation and disorder. Admittedly, it is very difficult to define how much stimulation is overstimulation. If infants have too many things around them to play with, touch, listen to, and look at, they may be overwhelmed, and they will not learn as effectively as with a proper balance of sameness and variability. Babies need the opportunity and time to think about and master new information, and this cannot be done with constant bombardment of new experiences. In a group care situation there will be a lot going on most of the time. Although it is important not to be overprotective, some babies who are very responsive to what is going on around them will need more protection than others. The caregiver, by being aware of the atmosphere and staying calm, quiet, and gentle during even the busiest times, can influence the atmosphere of the nursery to a large extent.

8. Babies should be kept from experiencing unduly severe or prolonged distress. Caregivers must be sensitive to distress and its signifi-

cance as an indicator of need, and must be capable of helping infants cope with the distress. Very young babies may need assistance in quieting themselves, and all babies need help and warm support in learning to manage distress. It is our position that adults responding to distress promptly and appropriately will help babies learn to manage their own distress, rather than use crying excessively to get what they want. This does not mean that a baby's distress should always lead immediately to getting what he or she wants. It does mean that crying is a legitimate way of communicating and that a baby should not be allowed to cry for a very long time or until he or she becomes hysterical and has great difficulty in being quieted.

9. Babies can begin to develop very early in life the attitude that learning is pleasurable. Caregivers can foster this attitude by their own enjoyment of caregiving and by exercising their capacity to show pleasure in learning. They should be aware of what is pleasurable to the baby and encourage babies' reactions. If learning is a pleasurable experience, more learning and exploration will take place. Also, learning to learn with pleasure involves a special kind of social interaction with the caregiver.

10. Infants enjoy and learn a great deal from interacting with

6

other infants. A quality day care program gives babies the opportunity to interact pleasurably with each other. For very young babies (nonmobile), this means frequently placing them near one another. At the same time, babies must be protected from each other as they begin to learn appropriate ways of interacting. Caregivers must have great patience as they care for older babies, who have to begin to learn some self-control, and who have, as yet, no understanding of sharing.

As we mentioned earlier, babies also need some opportunities to be alone. Spending all of their time as part of a group might encourage an excessive dependence on others for entertainment and help.

11. In order to do a good job, caregivers must enjoy their role. Enjoying babies is not sufficient— caregivers must also be able to work smoothly with each other and to communicate effectively. They also need appropriate relief time from caregiving—no one should be expected to do a good job as a caregiver for eight hours a day. Many people feel strongly that the most important component of a successful program is that the overall atmosphere is a warm, child-oriented one. This quality is difficult to train for; rather, it comes as a by-product of competent, caring individuals who enjoy children and are basically happy in their work setting.

One of the concerns of any program is how to ensure that caregivers continue to feel a sense of self-worth, competence, and enjoyment in their roles.

12. In a good day care program, there is consistency between day care and home caregiving practices. Consistency of care within the day care setting itself has already been mentioned. Moreover, caregivers must respect the parents' right to make decisions about the care of their baby and follow the parents' practices. Arrangements should be set up to assure that parents and caregivers can talk with each other daily about the baby. Caregivers need to know how the baby is cared for at home—for instance, the usual procedure before naptime, what foods the baby is eating—so that they can care for the baby in much the same way when he is away from home. Communication between parents and staff will make the job of caregiving easier and more pleasant, and most importantly, will lead to a more sensible, enjoyable experience for the baby. Parents should be given the opportunity to participate in the care of their baby in the day care program as much as is feasible. Encouraging parents to visit their baby in the program may lead to their participation. They should know that they influence the care of their baby in the program. The staff can play a very important role, especially with new parents, in giving support as well as information.

Chapter 1. Goals and Principles—Notes

1. The list contained in the text is a general one. For more detailed information on the specific skills and competencies of the two-year-old, the reader is referred to Chapter 5, note 3, which lists sources of information on normal development.

2. In recent years, a number of individuals, including the authors of this book, have developed statements of goals and principles of infant care in group settings. These principles reflect a good bit of general consensus despite variations in details:

Caldwell, B.M. "What Is the Optimal Learning Environment for the Young Child?" *America Journal of Orthopsychiatry* 37 (1967):8-21.

Huntington, D.S.; Provence, S.; and Parker, R.K. *Day Care 2: Serving Infants.* Washington, D.C.: U.S. Government Printing Office, 1971 [DHEW Publication No. (OCD) 72-8].

White, B.L. "Our Goals for the Infant and His Family." In *The Infants We Care For*, edited by L.L. Dittmann. Washington, D.C.: National Association for the Education of Young Children, 1973.

Two sets of slides are available which illustrate principles of good infant and toddler group care.

"But What Do You Do With Them?" Joan Johnston and Anne Willis, Cornell Infant Nursery. Available from Cornell Film Library, Roberts Hall, Cornell University, Ithaca, N. Y. 14853.

"Hidden Treasure," Infant Care Project, University of North Carolina at Greensboro, Greensboro, N. C. 27412.

Chapter 2

Relations with Families

Maintaining close relations between a group care program and the families it serves, referred to in the last principle in Chapter 1, is a very important matter which requires more detailed discussion.[1]* Any quality program for babies cannot be just for babies, but must involve the entire family. There is considerable variability, of course, in the amount and kinds of parent involvement associated with day care programs, depending on the nature and purpose of the center. Some programs may have parent education as a specific goal, and these will include a heavy emphasis on formal parent involvement, either as cooperative caregivers or as policymakers.[2] However, even a day care program whose primary aim does not go beyond providing quality day care for children cannot accomplish its goal without developing a good working relationship with the parents, both mother and father. Being supportive of parents, providing them with information, giving them the opportunity to have an influence on the kind of care their baby is receiving—in short, doing anything that will nourish and increase the parents' pleasure in their baby—should be an aim of all child care programs.

One of the most rewarding jobs

---

*Footnotes for this chapter are located on page 17.

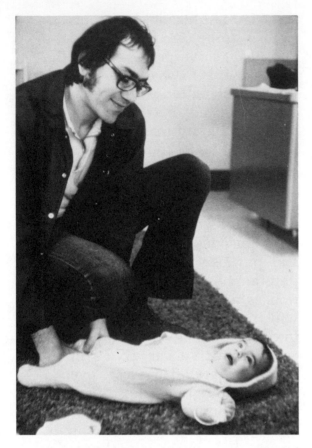

of the caregiver can be helping the parents become more aware of the baby's accomplishments, pointing out to them the child's expanding abilities—in short, helping them to enjoy their child's uniqueness more and discouraging them from excessive comparisons of their baby with other babies. In doing this, the caregiver is playing a very important teaching role. Maintaining a supportive, optimistic attitude during times when parents are worried about the baby's development will also be helpful.

One of the criticisms expressed about day care is that it weakens or

minimizes the importance of the family by taking responsibility for children away from parents and giving it to other people. While some kinds of day care may not contribute to the child's sense of belonging to the family and vice versa, *quality* day care necessarily includes working with the family to strengthen it. One of the goals for an infant day care program mentioned in the previous chapter is to help the baby begin to develop a strong sense of belonging to his or her family. This can be accomplished effectively by nourishing the parents' sense of belongingness to the baby. Caregivers should encourage parents to make decisions about the baby's care in the program and should discuss with them any problems or proposed changes in the baby's care. Even in fairly unimportant matters, caregivers should try to accommodate to parents' requests. For instance, a mother may feel strongly that her baby's food should be warmed before feeding. The caregiver should respect this wish, if it can be incorporated into the routine without too much disruption.

Sometimes parents of firstborns, particularly, will have to be encouraged to make decisions, for they might be very willing to have an experienced caregiver make most of the decisions about the baby's care—when to begin to serve table foods, for instance. Caregivers

10

certainly know the babies well, and often are more experienced than new parents in child care, but the wise caregiver will offer suggestions and give information tactfully and cautiously, being certain the distinction between facts and opinions is clear. A caregiver would also want to avoid ever giving the impression that she is an expert evaluating the parents' practices. It is often difficult for a caregiver not to offer unsolicited advice, but in most cases caregivers will wait until the parents open the way for discussion. For example, caregivers, aware of the current advice of pediatricians, might feel that shoes are not necessary or even appropriate for babies who are not walking in places where feet need protection. While they might remove the shoes of a six-month-old at the center, the issue is not serious enough to bring up with the parents. On the other hand, if a baby has had several unusual bowel movements, the caregiver might tactfully ask the parents what foods he has been getting at home and suggest some alternatives if the diet might be causing the problem.

Direct parental involvement should be facilitated and encouraged where feasible. If the center is located near their work, some parents may want to come during the day to feed or play with their baby. A place and opportunity to do this should be provided. Parent meet-ings on any of a number of topics offer another vehicle for helping both parents and day care staff become better caregivers.

Initial Contacts

Parents should be encouraged to visit a day care center and to observe its program before they decide it is right for their baby. During this time they should also have a chance to talk with the caregivers and ask questions. Before it is decided that a baby will participate in a program, the parents and caregivers should discuss what they expect of each other. The center's health regulations and policy regarding illness should be understood clearly. Misunderstandings about arrival and departure times, if they are not settled early, can result in an unpleasant relationship between parents and caregivers. At the end of the day, caregivers are tired and eager to go home. They are not likely to react pleasantly to a late parent who does not have a very good reason for being late. Bringing out these issues in the beginning, having both parents and caregivers ask questions of each other, lays the groundwork for a pleasant, open, supportive relationship. (An example of an information sheet is included in Appendix A.)

Daily Contacts

An important kind of parent involvement comes from exchanging information daily about the baby. It is helpful to both caregivers and parents to know about the baby's eating, sleeping, general health, and mood during the times they are not with him. (Two daily information sheets, one filled out by parents before bringing the baby in, and the other used by caregivers to record the baby's activities during the day, were used in the Cornell program; see Appendix A.) In the interest of facilitating home-to-nursery continuity in infant care, caregivers should make an effort to find out how the baby is taken care of at home by asking questions of the parents, and perhaps observing them caring for the baby at home. For example, it is important for caregivers to have an idea of the way parents usually show affection and soothe the baby. This sort of continuity in care is possible only to a degree, because the settings and the caregivers will be different. Sometimes, consistency can be easily established by parents keeping caregivers up-to-date on what is happening at home. For example, if a baby is learning to drink from a cup at home, informing the caregivers of this and asking them to use one in the nursery will make the learning process easier. Further, in working with families from different cultural backgrounds, there are likely to be childrearing customs that may be unfamiliar to caregivers. The importance of these

customs and the need to respect them should continuously be made clear to the caregivers.

It is probably not harmful for the baby to experience some diversity in care. However, naptime, eating routines, use of a pacifier, use of prohibitions, for instance, should be handled similarly in both settings as long as a caregiver does not feel that following a certain practice is clearly disadvantageous for the baby. If a practice is questioned, discussing the matter with the parents would be necessary. A baby will learn more efficiently if responded to in a similar way at home and in the nursery. For example, if a baby is biting other babies often in play, the caregiver might want to discuss this with the parents when it is convenient, to find out if it happens at home and what they do about it. This is an example of where consistent responses by adults at home and in the nursery are important in helping the baby to learn to guide his or her own behavior. While a father and mother might view playful biting as another kind of enjoyable play, other babies might not view it this way, and one would want to discourage it in the nursery. To further illustrate, a baby's mother might request that caregivers not pick up a baby who cries after being put down for a nap (especially if the baby has shown many signs of being tired), since she allows the

12

child to cry for up to fifteen or twenty minutes at home. Caregivers should agree to try this to see how it works. What is most important is that they be able to talk honestly and openly with the mother about the effectiveness of that strategy after they have tried it.

In answering questions and handling problems that arise, it is best for each caregiver to work directly with the parents of the babies in her care. It is possible that some caregivers may not get along particularly well with some parents because of personality differences or differences in background. This fact should be acknowledged and coped with in a way that will not adversely affect the care the baby is receiving, for instance, by changing primary caregivers, if possible. Part of the rationale for assigning babies to caregivers (to be discussed in Chapter 3) should be the caregiver's ability to get along and communicate well with that baby's parents.

Appropriate handling of babies' distress at separating from the parent is an issue that may arise even when babies are being left with a caregiver they know and trust. Some babies at around nine to twelve months of age have difficulties adjusting to being left. Caregivers need to respect this difficulty and discuss with parents the best ways of handling it. When parents are feeling ambivalent about parting and are making separation more difficult, for instance by encouraging very prolonged good-byes, the situation requires special sensitivity on the part of the caregiving staff. Again, knowledge of what has been happening at home can help parents, caregiver, and baby cope with such situations more effectively.

Sometimes considerable information concerning family circumstances is necessary in order to understand the baby's behavior and needs. Maintaining a sense of privacy and confidentiality is essential. (See Appendix A-1.)

The question of home visits— should they be made, who should make them, what is the purpose of them—must be answered by each individual program, given its specific goals. Information about the child's home life, what materials there are to play with, the child's sleeping arrangements, involvement with other family members, and what the child's behavior is like at home can be useful in helping the caregiver to be effective at the center. However, visits must be carefully handled. Parents should not be made to feel that they are being evaluated—a visit must be a mutually agreed upon exchange of information and should never be pressed upon a reluctant parent.

Entering and Leaving a Program

Very young babies (younger

13

than five months) are not likely to experience much difficulty in adjusting to a change from home care to a day care situation, since they are unlikely to have developed clear attachments to specific people or settings. However, with babies over five months old, some consideration should be given by parents and caregivers together to making their transitions to a new care situation easier. If possible, an older baby should be brought to a center at first for a short time with a parent or other familiar person, gradually lengthening the stay to a full day. The parents' involvement can be tapered off as the baby and caregiver become more comfortable with each other. It is very likely that the baby will show some changes in behavior that come from being in a new situation with a new caregiver. For instance, an older baby is likely to show some distress at being left by mother in a relatively new setting, and the adjustment may take several days.

In the same way, when a baby is going to leave a program because the family is moving or their situation is otherwise changing, parents and caregivers together should make plans to ensure a smooth transition for the baby. For some babies, decreasing gradually the amount of time spent at the center may be helpful, if the parents' schedules allow it. Arrangements will, of course, depend on the baby's needs and the circumstances surrounding the change, but the issue is one that deserves attention.[3]

Responsibility of Program to Parents

While the informal exchanges of information between parent and caregiver are important, it is also helpful for a group care program to be aware of specific responsibilities that it has to the parents. These include those that are implicit in any arrangement where one person is taking care of another person's child, as well as the possibility for optional services.

The responsibilities implicit in caring for another person's child include the following.

(1) The baby's health, safety, and general welfare will be the first consideration of the caregiver.

(2) The caregiver's concern extends *beyond* maintenance or custodial care of the baby, as important as that is, to meeting the child's social and emotional needs and providing interesting learning experiences.

(3) Caregiving practices will be consistent and reliable; that is, they will *not* change drastically from day to day. Major changes will be discussed and agreed upon by parents and caregivers.

(4) The caregiver will make an effort to find out as much as possible about the baby and how he or she is used to being taken care of at home. In so far as possible the caregiver will try to care for the baby in ways similar to those used at home, considering that the situation is different and the indivdual caregiver may have a different style than the parent.

(5) The caregiver will remember that the parents have major responsibility for the baby and should be the decision makers. This is an obvious fact that can sometimes be hard for caregivers to put into practice. Anyone who lives with a child for even part of the day on a regular basis develops a large investment in that child. The importance of the baby and caregiver establishing a warm and close relationship has been stressed. However, caregivers must guard against allowing a situation where parents and caregivers are vying for the baby's attention and affection. Responsibility and ultimate belongingness are the parents', and the caregiver must respect this, even though it may sometimes be difficult.

Additional Services to Parents

A program that is staffed and budgeted comfortably can perform additional services beyond infant care. A day care program is a good place for dissemination of information about all aspects of child care. Every staff member should be acquainted with resources in the community to meet special needs of families—social workers, medical specialists, nutritionists, counselors. Informal parent conferences with the caregivers should be set up on a regular basis. Often the parent or the caregiver might not initiate an encounter by suggesting that a conference be arranged, but if there is one regularly scheduled, they will have something to discuss.

A problem cannot be dealt with effectively in the home or day care center alone, but must be confronted in a consistent way in both settings. The caregiver has the responsibility to inform the parent in a tactful way of any of the child's behaviors that could develop into a problem, and together they should plan a course of action. It is not wise or even desirable that the caregiver should always burden the parent with a detailed account of the baby's day, if it has not been a good one. Being told how many times a baby cried, or pulled hair, or took a toy away from another child does not establish the perfect atmosphere for reuniting a tired child with a tired mother at the end of the day! If a mother seems unusually tired or irritable, the caregiver may decide to limit comments to only positive reports. Caregivers should always relate positive information, new accomplishments and landmarks, but be more selective in bringing up problems.

Parent meetings can serve many purposes at once, not the least of which is giving information to the parents on a wide range of topics, including nutrition, safety in toys, common illnesses in babies, current research in childrearing practices or day care, discipline problems with toddlers, and the role of the mother and father in the family. Meetings give the caregivers an opportunity to demonstrate their increasing competence and knowledge in areas of child care, and parents and caregivers can learn new attitudes as well as facts about caring for their children.

What is most important when parents and caregivers work together is something that cannot be established by writing it down on a list of responsibilities—namely, that an attitude of openness, of mutual concern for the baby, be established. Parents and caregivers should feel comfortable sharing any information that will help them to understand the baby better and provide more effective care.

In summary, a good day care center for babies is a family-centered one, representing a cooperative effort by parents and caregivers to provide a good experience for each baby.

Chapter 2. Relations with Families—Notes

1. Brazelton, T.B. "Working with the Family" In *The Infants We Care For*, edited by L.L. Dittmann. Washington, D.C.: National Association for the Education of Young Children, 1973.

2. A good example of programs concerned primarily with helping low-income families to optimize the health and general development of their children under the age of three is represented by the Parent and Child Development Centers, supported by the Office of Child Development, Department of Health, Education, and Welfare (originally under the aegis of the Office of Economic Opportunity). Several of these centers are involved in extensive research and demonstration activities to evaluate the effectiveness of programs which involve a combination of day care center experience for parents and children, and a home visiting parenting education component. Recent descriptions of this program are contained in the following references.

Pechman, S.M. "Seven Parent and Child Centers." *Children Today* 1 (1972):28-31.

Work, H.H. "Parent-Child Centers: A Working Reappraisal." *American Journal of Orthopsychiatry* 42 (1972):582-595.

3. An attempt was made in the Cornell nursery in the summer of 1972 to "wean" babies from the program in a somewhat systematic way, by decreasing gradually either the number of days each week or the number of hours each day that babies spent in the program. An informal assessment consisted of parents' opinions of the effects on their baby's behavior. A brief report is available from the authors of the book.

Chapter 3

Program and Staff Organization

Attention is next directed to a number of general considerations, in addition to working with families, that affect the overall operation of the program and the daily activities of the caregivers. These considerations all relate directly or indirectly to individualizing care, to building a group program based on sensitive caring for each baby. Four issues will be discussed: assigning caregivers to babies, appropriate ratio of caregivers to babies, optimal group size, and age range in the group.

Assigning Caregivers to Babies

Having caregivers assign themselves primary responsibility for the babies they are to care for serves many purposes.[1]* In the beginning of a program, it allows each caregiver to narrow her scope somewhat, to concentrate on getting to know a few babies rather than the entire group. As the principal caregiver for a particular baby, she is the one who talks with the parents at the beginning and end of the day, feeds the baby, and as much as possible is the main person who interacts with the baby. This arrangement not only facilitates this specific caregiver becoming an "expert" on that baby, but also helps the baby to adapt to the new situation. The child learns to

---

*Footnotes for this chapter are located on pages 26-27.

expect certain kinds of responses and gets used to a new style of caregiving. In short, the baby learns to make sense of his or her world more easily when it is predictable and consistent. Getting to know one new caregiver at a time is easier than getting used to two or three simultaneously. The arrangement must, of course, be a flexible one. Getting to know and trust all of the caregivers is important for the baby, too, since the principal caregiver will not be accessible all the time, and in reality, all caregivers will eventually care for all babies. If a baby needs to be rocked, for example, whoever is free should rock him or her. When there is a choice, however, and especially when a

baby is new to a program, he or she should be cared for by his or her principal caregiver. Long after the babies feel comfortable with all the caregivers, and each caregiver knows all of the babies very well, the caregiver's feeling of being *the* authority on a baby, of being the person in the program who knows the child best and to whom he or she "belongs," seems to last. And some babies do continue to show a preference for their principal caregiver.

Caregivers themselves should make the decisions about which babies they are assigned to. They will base that decision on compatibility between themselves and the baby as well as the baby's parents

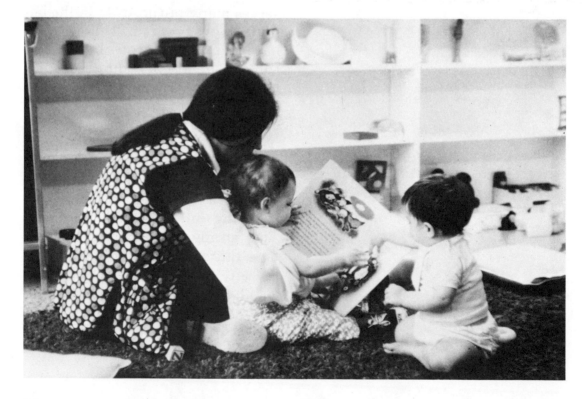

20

and the degree to which the baby is difficult or easy to care for. If there are several babies in a group who demand a lot of caregiving time, they should be assigned to different caregivers.

The development of a special relationship between caregiver and baby is stressed throughout this book. Caregivers must remain aware of two issues related to this—the possibility of overattachment, and the focussing of attention selectively on favorite babies. It is to be expected that certain babies and caregivers will be attracted to each other because of compatibility of personalities and styles. Every caregiver has her own style and pace of interacting, and babies may have preferences. Some babies react more positively to a vigorous, intense style with a lot of movement and talking, for instance, while others prefer a quieter, more casual, gentler kind of handling. Caregivers should accept objectively the fact that some babies will react more favorably to them than others.

Caregivers may become very attached to babies and may take great pleasure when certain babies show affection preferentially for them. The caregiver must at all times have in mind the baby's best interests and healthy development. It would not be adaptive for a baby to become overly attached to or dependent upon a single staff member, so that the baby could not be happy when they are apart. Self-reliance and a generalized trust that comes from a relationship with a few trusted individuals are the goals to be worked for.

As for caregivers having "favorite" babies, it is inevitable that certain babies are at times more attractive than others. Luckily, different adults are attracted to different characteristics in babies, and babies change over time, so that a baby who is especially responsive and appealing now may be less so in a few weeks. However, some babies are generally more active, outgoing, and responsive than others, and they can soon become the obvious "stars" in a group. Having favorites is inevitable. The best way to cope with this is to be aware of it and work against it by trying harder to find special qualities in quieter, less responsive babies.

Ratio of Caregivers to Babies

Many state licensing agencies specify ratios of caregivers to babies in day care programs. This is another area where recommendations are contingent on a number of factors which will vary in each center. Also, the ideal arrangements may not be possible. In general, one caregiver for every four babies between the ages of two and twelve to fourteen months is adequate if there is extra help available during busy times of the day. The extra help can come from parents, a few volunteers, or a "floating" caregiver, but it should be someone who knows the babies and with whom the babies are familiar. After babies in a group program put themselves on some kind of schedule, it becomes possible to predict the busy times when extra help is needed. These will very likely be around feeding time in the middle of the day. The extra help may be someone to hold and rock a fussy baby, someone to prepare lunches, or someone to play with a baby. Especially in a group where there are several very young babies, one caregiver for every four babies is not adequate staffing without additional help.

Experience in the Cornell program leads to the conclusion that a better situation is a one-to-three ratio of caregivers to babies. The caregivers in the Cornell Nursery found there was a period of approximately three months, when most of the babies were between seven and ten months old, that they felt very comfortable having major responsibility for four babies. Younger babies need an amount of holding and close one-to-one contact that a one-to-four ratio will not allow. Similarly, older babies (around a year old) are beginning to be ready for play experiences that often require more planning and help from an adult, again making a one-to-three ratio desirable.

Programs must be cautious in relying on volunteers to improve the caregiver-to-baby ratio. While a few volunteers working on a regular basis can be helpful in improving the quality of the program, involving many different people who do not know the babies and are not known by them will create an unpleasant experience for all concerned. The importance of babies being cared for by a few individuals they come to know and trust has been stressed many times. The advantages of having extra people to give care must be weighed against the importance of having very few people involved in providing care.

Optimal Group Size

Having reached the decision that the ideal situation is one where each caregiver assumes primary responsibility for three babies, one is still left with the question of the optimal number of caregivers and babies that should consititute a group. In some cases, the total amount of physical space, the way it is divided, and the ages and numbers of children to be served determine group size. However, there are other factors which are equally as important.

Two extreme situations will provide a context for thinking about group size.

(A) Center A is located in a large old house with five small bedrooms upstairs. The total

group of fifteen babies is divided into five groups of three babies, each group having its own caregiver and its own equipment, and functioning autonomously in one of the five rooms.

(B) Center B is housed in a school building. Because there are twenty-one babies enrolled in the center, the infant program is assigned to the school gymnasium. Seven caregivers are hired.

Without substantial spatial reorganization, neither of these situations has much potential for becoming the kind of quality program described in these guidelines, for reasons indicated below.

Above and beyond interacting with individual babies, a caregiver must also see herself as responsible for the group as a whole. An awareness of what is going on all over the room must be maintained, even when there are other caregivers in the room. A caregiver must never become so engrossed in an activity that she loses sight of the general atmosphere as well as what each baby is doing. The general tone of the room, the noise level, the number of toys strewn around the floor, the number of adults present, and the degree of confusion or order can have a great effect on the contentment of each baby. For these reasons, it would not be recommended that large numbers of babies, even with an adequate number of caregivers and sufficient physical space, be cared for all together, as is the case in Center B. The potential for a noisy, disorganized, confusing atmosphere increases with the size of the group.

It was stated above that even though caregivers assign themselves primary responsibility for certain babies, they will, in reality, be sharing in the care of all the babies in the group. To care for each baby effectively and sensitively, a caregiver must know the baby well. It is doubtful that one caregiver could ever get to know twenty-one babies. Similarly, from the babies' point of view, getting to know seven new adults and adjusting to their styles of caregiving would be extremely difficult and would at best delay the baby's adjusting to the new situation.

On the other hand, a recommended minimum size for a group would be at least five to eight babies, with two caregivers, rather than the situation described in Center A. Adults caring for babies need other adults to talk with, to share accomplishments and frustrations with, if they are to do a

good job. It is much easier for a caregiver working with someone else to maintain enthusiasm and interest in caring for babies than when working alone. Also, if there is only one adult caring for even a small number of babies, she cannot leave the room easily. This is not a workable situation. Therefore, it would not be recommended that a group of eight babies and two caregivers, for instance, be divided into two groups of four babies with one caregiver each.

It has been our experience at Cornell that a group of eight to ten babies between the ages of eight weeks and one year is about the maximum number that a caregiving staff can get to know well. Ten babies would require a maximum of three caregivers for the babies to become acquainted with. A smaller group also adds the advantage of facilitating the babies' getting to know each other more easily. A group larger than ten children should be subdivided into several smaller, self-contained groups.

Age Range in Groups

Including babies of somewhat different ages in a group provides variety in the kinds of interactions and responsibilities caregivers have and gives babies opportunities to learn new skills from one another. For these reasons, even if staff arrangements, size of program, equipment, and physical space

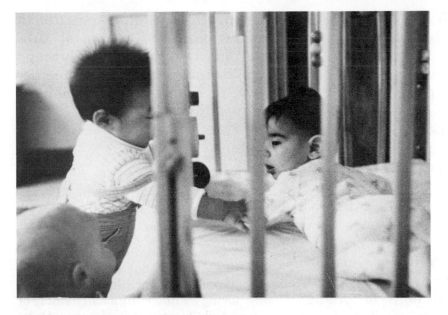

allow it, dividing a group of babies into narrow groups based on age or abilities (sitters, crawlers, walkers, for instance) is not recommended.

Guidelines for grouping children of varying ages cannot be given rigidly, and should be based on the combination of competencies needed to function effectively in a program designed for a particular group. Babies will attain these competencies at somewhat different ages; therefore, using a set age or a single skill, such as walking, as the criterion for moving children from one group to another is much less desirable than considering each baby's overall development and readiness for certain kinds of experiences. However, if babies vary widely in interests and skills, it is impossible to plan a single program that will meet their needs.

In many programs, a major distinction is made between *infants* younger than fifteen to eighteen months of age and *toddlers,* children approximately eighteen months to three years old. This dividing point is a valid one, for at around eighteen months of age there are major changes in children's competencies in several areas—for example, language production increases rapidly, and increased mobility is achieved with ease.

However, the experience in the Cornell Nursery suggests that within the age range that this book is concerned with (two to fifteen months), there are some important considerations relating to age grouping that would suggest grouping babies younger than twelve months of age separately from those older than twelve months. There are several developmental changes that occur around the first birthday that have implications for changing play experiences and also for planning of the total program: an increase in language comprehension, mobility, greater self-assertion, the beginnings of true social interaction with peers, for instance (see Chapter 5).

If a program is staffed adequately, a group of babies distributed in age between two and twelve to fourteen months can be a very pleasant, interesting situation for both caregivers and babies. It is possible to include both very young babies and younger walkers in a single group. However, in a group that includes older and younger babies together, three interrelated potential problems must be guarded against: (1) younger babies must be protected from older mobile babies; (2) the routine care of younger babies—feeding and holding, for instance—must not take up so much of the caregivers' time that they have little time for the older babies; (3) conversely, the relative ease and enjoyment of playing and interacting with responsive older babies should not keep caregivers from ensuring that younger babies are spending their time well. While a group of babies distributed fairly evenly in age between two months and one year is a workable situation, if a group included a cluster of very young babies (two to four months) and another cluster of older ones (ten to twelve months), a natural subgrouping into two smaller groups would occur some of the time because of differences in schedules and needs.

Chapter 3. Program and Staff Organization—Notes

1. Many of the suggestions in this chapter stem from our previously mentioned concern (Principle 2, Chapter 1) with having a sufficiently small number of different adults responsible for the infants' care, with sufficient stability and continuity, so that the babies might readily come to recognize their particular caregivers and develop appropriate feelings of confidence, trust, and affection for them. The two references listed below present the results of a longitudinal study of our 1971-72 infants' changing reactions to their caregivers and to strangers over the period when they were three to twelve months of age. These studies indicate quite clearly that the familiar nursery caregivers play a significant role in facilitating the infants' daily separations from home to the day care center and in helping infants to cope with typical fearful situations—in short, the familiar caregivers become significant alternate attachment figures for the infant.

Ricciuti, H.N. "Fear and the Development of Social Attachments in the First Year of Life." In *Origins of Human Behavior: Fear*, edited by M. Lewis and L. Rosenblum. New York: John Wiley and Sons, 1974.

This technical report also includes results of several pilot studies of the influence of extended day care experience in the first year of life on infants' responses to new social situations involving brief maternal separations.

Ricciuti, H.N., and Poresky, R.H. "Development of Attachment to Caregivers in an Infant Nursery during the First Year of Life." Paper presented at meetings of the Society for Research in Child Development, March 1973, Philadelphia, Pa.

This is a briefer, less technical report on infants' attachment to caregivers.

A very good discussion of the more general issue of the development of social attachment between infant and mother, along with a consideration of implications for social policy and practice, is contained in the following work.

Ainsworth, M.D.S. "The Development of Infant-Mother Attachment." In *Review of Child Development Research, Vol. 3. Child Development and Social Policy*, edited by B.M. Caldwell and H.N. Ricciuti. Chicago: University of Chicago Press, 1973.

Chapter 4

The Program: A Caregiver's Day

We now turn to a detailed consideration of the specifics of good caregiving practices, viewed from the perspective of what happens in the nursery, how it happens, and to some extent, why it happens. Clearly, it is much easier to list caregiving principles than to ensure that they are acted upon consistently. This chapter and the three that follow represent a translation of principles and philosophy into what takes place each day in the nursery. A brief overview of a day in the nursery from the perspective of a caregiver offers an introductory context for later, more detailed discussion of specific areas of caregiving.[1]* The following description, as well as the other examples in the book, are, for the most part, taken from interactions between babies and caregivers in the Cornell program.

The caregiver's day begins before the babies arrive. Diapering and feeding equipment for the morning must be set up. She assists the caregiver she works with in putting linens on the cribs. The babies' favorite toys are set up, but some new toys are also put out. As each of the babies and parents arrive, they are greeted warmly. The caregiver receives the daily information

---

*Footnotes for this chapter are located on page 33.

sheet, and talks with the parent. The topics may range from the interesting thing the baby did yesterday, the fact that he or she woke up three times during the night, what should be served for lunch, to what toys seem to be liked best right now. When the parent leaves, the caregiver talks or plays briefly with the baby, then puts the child down and helps him or her begin to play by showing a toy. The caregiver must remain free to greet the other babies in much the same way.

When there is a pause, the first order of business is a diaper change for every baby. Noticing a slight rash on one baby's stomach, the caregiver calls the other caregiver over. They decide that it may be a reaction to a new food. A note of it is made to help remember to mention it to the parents. On the basis of the parent's report, the baby's typical

schedule, and the baby's behavior, the caregiver decides that one baby will probably play a while contentedly, another would like juice before a nap, still another is ready for a nap now, while another has not had breakfast and will be in a much better mood after some cereal and fruit. Caregivers seldom have the opportunity to do only one thing at a time. This is not to say that a baby never gets a caregiver's full attention, for it is very important that this happen for part of each day. What it does mean is that the caregiver, while being tuned in to what she is doing, must also have an awareness of what is happening with all the babies assigned to her. Anticipation of a baby's boredom or frustration before they occur gives the opportunity to try to prevent their occurrence.

The caregiver notices that two of the babies on the floor are interested in the same toy and are not willing to play with it together. She sits down on the floor between them, gives one of them another toy, and plays with them both for a time, then lays the sleepy baby in bed on his stomach and pats his back gently, remembering that his mother said that is what she does at home. When he is settled down, she prepares the fruit and cereal and places an older baby in a feeding table. While she is holding one baby and giving her cereal, she sits near and offers encouragement and

30

help to the baby who is learning to drink juice from a cup with a lid and spout. She talks and smiles occasionally to the baby playing busily on the floor.

Noticing that a baby seemed a bit bothered earlier by the other babies, the caregiver leaves her in the feeding table after she has finished her juice so that she can play quietly by herself. The caregiver brings over a cup and some cubes and encourages the baby to pick them up, showing her how to bang them together. The caregiver writes on the information sheet for parents what the babies ate.

The caregiver is now free to play with the babies. She places the two babies on the floor near each other, changing one from a sitting position to prone, and places the one who has just been fed in an infant seat. She then takes the orange clutch ball, raises it high in the air, squeezes it to get their attention, then lets it fall with a great flourish. The older baby looks around for it, so she waits to give him a chance to find it. When his eyes catch it, both caregiver and baby laugh with his success. This goes on for quite a while with many variations—covering the ball with a blanket and letting the baby uncover it, holding it in front of the younger baby and encouraging her to reach for it. The game also has the attention of the baby in the feeding table. The caregiver senses that she

is ready to come out, and asks, "Would you like to get out now?", emphasizing the "out," and before she extends her arms to pick her up, the baby's arms are raised in anticipation. The baby has begun to crawl recently and she is interested in practicing this most of her awake time. The caregiver knows this, and appreciates that she can move more freely now that some of the babies are sleeping. She may not have a chance to hold this baby on her lap for more than a few minutes, for the baby just does not have time for that, but she understands and will not push her to conform. The baby likes to be talked to, however, so the caregiver will talk to her many times during the day.

One of the babies on the floor is becoming very fussy, rubbing her eyes, and ignoring the toys around her. The caregiver picks her up and rocks her in the rocking chair while singing to her. When she seems relaxed and is almost asleep, the caregiver places her in her bed. Returning to the playroom, she notices that the other baby on the floor is trying very hard to move, straining to get a toy that is just out of reach, and having very little success. She watches for a time, then goes over and helps him give himself a little push. When he reaches the toy, she claps and praises him. They work together on moving for a few minutes. She sees that he is getting tired and frustrated, so she

31

takes a book from the shelf, puts the baby on her lap, and they "read" it together. She points to the pictures, talking about each one. She lets the baby turn the pages. Meanwhile, she is warming his bottle. She calls to the crawler, who is attempting to pull herself up to stand by holding on to the diaper pail. The call does not distract her from her endeavor, so the caregiver gets up, placing the baby she is holding on the floor, removes the other baby, and moves the diaper pail to a safer location. She places the baby who has been crawling in the jump chair for a few minutes, something this baby always enjoys. The bottle is warm, so she gives it to the baby, holding him in the rocking chair. He does not want it and lets her know by crying very loudly and vigorously. She tries several times without success, lays the bottle aside, holds him so that he can see her face, talks to him in a soothing way. Eventually he quiets, but starts crying again as she puts him in his crib. She leaves, thinking he may quiet himself, but after five minutes he is still crying, so she brings him back out into the playroom. He begins to play contentedly with the toys and stops crying. So much for a nap!

If she is lucky, the caregiver may have a short time for a break when most of the babies are napping. At least she may have time to relax and talk with the caregiver she works with. As the babies get up, some will be ready for lunch, and for them a diaper change seems interminably long. Others will be content to play for a time and wait their turn. Feeding time is one of the best times during the day. The caregiver should be relaxed, take time to talk with the baby, and let the child help if he or she wants to. On some days she may feed two babies at once, and this can be done in a pleasurable way for all involved. Today, however, she will be able to feed each one individually. She gets everything ready, including the peas that one mother requested she try for the first time with her baby. She takes over an extra spoon and a damp washcloth, anticipating that the baby, as he indicated yesterday, is interested in helping. There is much conversation over lunch. The caregiver helps the baby guide the spoon to the dish and then up to his mouth. Much of the food ends up on the table, but that is okay. A quick clean-up and the baby is ready to play again. . . .

So goes the caregiver's day. She takes a big break in the middle of the day for her lunch and to have a rest from her demanding job. The afternoon brings more of the morning's activities, except there is likely to be more irritability and fussiness because the babies are not as fresh. At the end of the day the caregiver will speak to the parents again, telling them about the baby's day in a way that increases their pleasure at being with their baby. She is aware that departure time at the end of the day, when adults and babies are tired, is sometimes unsettling. She tries to keep the babies occupied and relaxed while they wait for their parents. It is difficult sometimes to remember at the end of a busy day that during the morning one of the babies accomplished clapping his hands together in a deliberate way with great pleasure for the first time, or that another baby made the caregiver's job much less difficult by waiting very patiently for a late lunch during a time when the other babies were being very demanding. The caregiver knows, however, that these anecdotes are as important to relate to parents at the end of the day as information about eating and sleeping. She makes a point of remembering each day something special that each baby did to tell the parents. The caregiver's attitude about the baby can help a tired parent be happy to be with a tired baby at the end of the day. After saying good-bye to each of her babies, the caregiver straightens the room, putting things in order for the next day.

Somewhat simplified, this account depicts a *good* day, and not all days are that way. Essentially the program is defined by the way the caregivers meet these very concrete daily concerns. In the following chapters, the principles of good care for babies are interwoven among the concrete details of how to provide that care on a day-to-day basis.

**Chapter 4. The Program:
A Caregiver's Day—Notes**

1. A good overview of a caregiver's daily concerns is contained in:
Huntington, D.S.; Provence, S.; and Parker, R.K. *Day Care 2: Serving Infants.* Washington, D.C.: U.S. Government Printing Office, 1971 [DHEW Publication No. (OCD) 72-8.] See pp. 41-47.

Chapter 5

Play and Learning

In the first draft of this book, this chapter was entitled "Playtime." The implication, however, that playtime is a distinguishable part of the day in a group program for babies, like feeding time and naptime, is misleading. On the contrary, play, learning, and exploration are interwoven in the baby's total experience; thus virtually every chapter in this book is in some way concerned with play. This chapter, however, deals primarily with babies' activities at times other than during maintenance routines (for example, feeding, diapering, getting ready for a nap, changing clothes), with special emphasis on the role of the caregiver in the baby's learning, exploration, and play.

The definition of play in the first year of life must be broad, for play encompasses a wide range of encounters with the physical and social worlds. As discussed in this book, play includes *any* spontaneous pleasurable interaction with objects or people. Play can be almost anything—trying to climb in a rocking chair, exploring the construction of an infant seat, crawling over a big floppy pillow, watching what is going on in the room, beating a pot with a spoon, feeling another baby's toes, smiling back at a caregiver, clapping—the list could go on and on.

One of the most important features of play at any age is that much

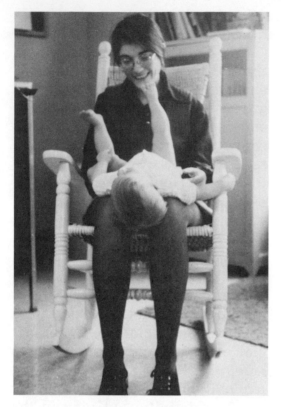

of it should be active, although it must be remembered that babies, like older people, can also learn by watching and listening. The quality of the infant's early play experiences, including both active exploration with hands and feet as well as quieter visual exploration, is critically important both for the infant's well-being at the time and for later development, since more advanced and complex skills are built on these early basic ones. Play experiences in the first year lay the groundwork for developing both curiosity about the world and positive attitudes toward other people. The beginnings of a sense of mastery and self-confidence come from

such experiences, and are the goals for play in the first year of life.[1]*

There are many ways of categorizing play experiences, and most of them are somewhat artificial since they isolate components of play that in reality occur together. The following examples of play activities fit into several categories simultaneously and include both active and quiet play, indoor and outdoor activities.

(1) *Social interaction*—sitting with the caregiver and watching her face as she talks or sings, talking to adults, looking and smiling at a baby nearby, playing "give it—take it back" with a caregiver or baby, communicating by pointing and babbling.

(2) *Language activities*—listening to the caregiver talk, babbling and cooing, saying long series of "da-da-da's," matching a word that the caregiver says to the object it belongs to (getting the ball from the toy shelf when the caregiver says, "Where is the *ball*?").

(3) *Perceptual-cognitive activities*—searching for a missing object, exploring the room visually, feeling the wind

---

*Footnotes for this chapter are located on pages 69-71.

outside, looking for a dropped rattle, "reading" a book with the caregiver, putting a shape through the correct slot in the sorting box, listening to the birds.

(4) *Large motor activities* —crawling, walking, learning to sit alone, climbing, chasing or being chased by another baby.

(5) *Small motor activities* —reaching, grasping small objects, playing pat-a-cake, stacking blocks, putting something into a container.

Social play, or the opportunity to interact pleasurably with adults in a variety of ways, is the single most important kind of play, for through it the baby can learn that other people are trustworthy, responsive, and fun to be with. Even the most colorful, most enjoyable, most educational play materials cannot by themselves provide the experiences gained from being with other people. **The use of play materials as a substitute for social interaction must be guarded against, although it is important for babies to learn to be independent, to be comfortable exploring**

the world by themselves. Interesting play materials, thoughtfully chosen, can both encourage interactions with other people and also provide occasions for exploring and learning alone. The caregiver, therefore, functions in two ways: most importantly, she interacts directly with the baby, both initiating play and responding to the baby's overtures; secondly, she sets up the physical environment in which the baby plays and provides opportunities for the baby to explore and discover alone.

Following this introductory section there are discussions of several general guidelines relating to all play. Attention is then directed to more detailed discussions of social play involving adults and babies together, play materials, and a brief consideration of babies playing with other babies.

Play and Learning as Natural Experiences

The baby of any age brings to the play situation certain capabilities, interests, and an unbridled curiosity about the world. Those people who plan and participate in play experiences with babies, whether as parents, caregivers in day care, or "infant educators," should be concerned with nourishing these existing and emerging interests and competencies, primarily by encouraging spontaneous and natural play. Such an approach is preferable to concentrating on artificially scheduled activities or exercises with the goal of speeding up normal development. This, of course, does not mean that babies should be left entirely on their own to provide themselves with the play experiences they need. Rather, it means that caregivers should encourage play as an integral part of the infants' daily experience, occurring spontaneously and naturally in interaction with the world. It is not necessary, for example, to set up many special exercises to give young babies experience in viewing objects from different perspectives; that happens frequently in the natural course of each day. On the other hand, it is important that caregivers be aware of visual following as an emerging skill in young babies, so that they can identify the opportunities they are providing for the baby to practice it. Babies' interests will—and should—determine their activities to a greater extent than any prescribed list. Babies sometimes seem to become "obsessed" with a particular kind of play, usually an emerging motor skill. A baby learning to crawl, for instance, may be interested only in crawling for a few days. Such a baby will not be dissuaded from this activity, even by the most attractive toy, and should be allowed to pursue this interest.

The best way to sensitize people to play effectively with babies is to provide them with general guidelines made meaningful with specific examples of age-appropriate activities, information on how babies develop in the first year of life, and help in becoming aware of the particular styles, interests, and competencies of individual babies. Part of our definition of play is that it is enjoyable—in order to meet that description it must be baby-centered, not activity-centered. **The problem with formal structured curricula is that they sometimes emphasize activities over babies.** They frequently fail to take into account individual differences in the capabilities and interests of babies of the same age. There is nothing inherently wrong with planning particular activities, but more than a list of specific activities is necessary to have a good program. Weikart and Lambie's concept of curriculum is very close to our own. A curriculum's main purpose, in their view, is to provide teachers, caregivers, or parents with a rationale for doing what they do with babies. In that sense, a set of beliefs about what babies are like, how development in the first year proceeds, and how it can be aided constitutes a curriculum.[2] The twelve principles that form the core of this book, therefore, represent the basis of our curriculum.

Normal Development and Individual Differences

The assumption implicit in this discussion of play is that caregivers have some knowledge of infant development in the first year and, therefore, a sense of what kinds of play experiences are appropriate for babies at different developmental levels.[3] It is especially important that caregivers know about the usual order of developmental changes if they are to be sensitive to emerging capabilities in the babies (Appendix B). It is equally important that they become attuned to individual differences in interests, capabilities, and styles of play among babies of the same age.[4]

It hardly needs to be said that during the first year of life many changes occur in the way babies interact with the world. Caregivers must adapt to these changes, both in selecting play materials and in interacting with the babies. For instance, a very young baby enjoys and learns from being placed in a spot where he or she can see what is going on in the room. Long before the baby is mobile—even before using hands to reach for and grasp objects—he or she explores by looking and listening, and a good vantage point gives the opportunity to follow people visually, to associate sounds and their sources. A sensitive caregiver will be sure to put a two- or three-month-old in such a place much of the time.

In general, the older a baby is, the easier it is to know how to play with him or her, largely because the baby becomes more a participant and less an observer. Play becomes more an exchange between two people and less a presentation by an adult. It is also true, however, that as babies get older, they become more capable of entertaining themselves. Caregivers need to be aware of this in caring for a group of young children of different ages, for the natural tendency might be to spend more time than is appropriate with the older babies and less with the younger ones.

Play with younger babies usu-ally needs to be more deliberate, more carefully planned, than that with older babies. Younger babies, with less understanding and more limited experience than older babies, need play with some protection from large numbers of disturbing, unexpected occurrences. To draw a nine-month-old's attention to a ball, for example, the caregiver needs only to hold it up and call the baby's name. It is very likely that the baby, if interested, will reach out for it or crawl over to get it. With a two-month-old, the caregiver may need to put the object in the baby's line of vision, move it slowly and regularly, and perhaps talk to the baby to draw attention to the object.

Stability in the General Environment

If a baby is to have the kinds of play experiences discussed in this chapter, there must be a reasonable consistency in the people, the physical set-up, and the routines that make up each baby's daily experience. In other words, there must be a sense of basic stability which provides a secure background for the day-to-day variations that occur naturally. This is one way in which the issue of an appropriate balance of variety and sameness in the environment, Principle 4 (see Chapter 1), is relevant to a discussion of play.

This background stability facilitates play in two ways. First, interaction with a warm, responsive adult who knows the baby is the single most important factor in a baby's play. An adult must spend a lot of time with a baby in order to get to know the baby's style, interests, and competencies. The second role that a predictable, secure environment plays is that of freeing the baby to explore, to be curious, to get involved in play. If a baby must react and adjust constantly to new caregivers, new babies, new routines, new equipment or room arrangement, the day will be spent coping with these changes. No baby can feel secure in an environment in which the major predictable aspect is that there are many and frequent changes! Having the same caregivers, keeping the composition of the group of babies somewhat stable, carrying out routines in somewhat the same way each day, having caregivers react similarly in disciplining babies, using the same verbal labels for familiar objects—all of these factors together contribute to consistency.

Sameness and Variety in Daily Activities

A second consideration with regard to the appropriate balance of sameness and variety relates specifically to how the baby is spending time in the program and the variety of opportunities for play that the caregiver provides. Whereas in the discussion above, sameness referred to consistency in the overall setting as a backdrop for good play, in the present context, sameness means "doing the same familiar activities" as opposed to "doing something new and different." **Play**

should be a combination of exploring new objects, practicing new skills, meeting new challenges, and enjoying the ease of using a skill already mastered, the comfortable feeling of re-exploring the familiar.[5] It is easy to overlook the value of repeating or reviewing the familiar in consolidating old skills and acquiring new ones. What sometimes appear to adults as boring, repetitious activities may be very important for cementing skills that have recently been acquired. An eleven-month-old may spend ten or fifteen minutes putting objects into a can and taking them out again. A sensitive caregiver will see the importance of this activity and will not interfere to change it.

Especially in the area of motor development, babies seem to need time to consolidate new skills after they have initially learned them. It is as though after practicing and working hard, the baby takes great delight in the new accomplishment and wants to spend considerable time doing it over and over. Also, babies who are learning a new skill in one area may need the security and self-confidence that come from doing other easy, familiar activities. A twelve-month-old struggling to walk may spend much nonwalking time cuddling stuffed toys or banging blocks, making good use of resting time.

Babies differ greatly in their ability to adapt to change, as well as in how much variety and novelty they need to stay interested and happy. One baby, for instance, will adapt almost immediately to the change from vigorously jumping up and down on the caregiver's lap, accompanied by laughter and talking, to being quietly rocked and sung to. This baby will settle down quickly, seeming to enjoy the contrast. Another baby will need a much more gradual transition from jumping to quieter activity. Sensitive caregivers will adjust accordingly the way they interact with a particular baby.

The best guide to how much sameness and variety are appropriate in play is the particular baby's own reactions. If he or she seems bored, disinterested, uninvolved, fussy, then perhaps new opportunities should be provided. The available toys might be too difficult and therefore frustrating, too easy and therefore boring, or appropriate for the baby's developmental level but uninteresting because they are not novel. If caregivers put toys away for a time, interest in them may be renewed when they are brought out again. Similarly, rearranging the furniture can create new areas to explore. A baby needs choices in play activities, but if he or she is very distractible, fussy, or unable to settle down to an activity, it may mean that there are too many choices. It is a difficult job for the caregiver, especially when playing with a younger baby, to keep pace with the baby's short attention span, to drop what she thinks should be an engaging activity because the baby is exhibiting a lack of interest. And although the baby's level of involvement and mood are the best cues about the appropriate balance of sameness and variety, it is probably safe to say that if the caregiver is tired of presenting a particular toy or playing peek-a-boo, it is very likely that it is time for a change.

Caregivers must make judgments continually about when to introduce new experiences. A good general guideline to follow is that **if the baby appears to be getting something out of an activity in terms of his or her repertoire of competencies, then there is no great need to change or add activities.** For example, a four-month-old trying to seize a toy swinging slowly in front of him could be allowed to pursue this activity (and given help if he becomes frustrated), since he is actively improving his skill in visually guided reaching. But a four-month-old who is "locked into" simply looking at a mobile or design out of reach for long periods of time probably is not spending her time as constructively, since she is capable of doing much more than simply staring at an interesting object.

Caregivers should be especially aware of how younger babies are spending their time. They should provide appropriate variety in stimulation, perhaps by changing the infant's position—turning them over, sitting them up, or moving them from crib to floor. Older babies, especially as they become able to sit up and move around, have some control over the amount of sameness and variety in their day. In the day care environment, presumably there will be many choices of activities, some novel, some more familiar.

As caregivers concern themselves with introducing appropriate changes, they may find it useful to view changes as belonging to one of two categories: first, those that are suggested just for the sake of variety, to prevent boredom; second, those that are designed to "stretch" the baby in some way, to offer a challenge.

The Importance of Challenges

Providing both sameness and variety in the baby's daily play experiences can be viewed as giving the opportunity to consolidate *and* to stretch. "Stretching" experiences, or challenges, occur any time the baby is confronted with the opportunity to do or understand something that demands cognitive, motor, social, or communication skills that have not yet been mastered completely. Challenges may also be viewed as problems to solve.

Many challenges occur naturally, but caregivers should be sure that appropriate challenges are a part of the baby's daily play experiences.[6]

If a challenging activity is to serve the purpose of encouraging the baby to develop a new skill, it must be based on what he or she already knows or can do. Development proceeds in an orderly way; new skills are based on old ones, complex behaviors come after their simpler components. New experiences should be built on previous ones. As mentioned earlier, babies should not be rushed but should be given the opportunity to master new skills at their own rate. For example, as soon as the baby has mastered a form board with circles, to remove that immediately and introduce a more difficult one with squares and triangles is to deny the pleasure of using a skill already mastered as well as the practice needed to consolidate the skill. Similarly, a caregiver would not introduce variations of similar challenging activities while the baby is mastering them. For instance, a caregiver would not in the same play session introduce the baby both to stacking blocks and to inserting them in a sorting box. Similarly, if the caregiver were trying to teach an eight-month-old seated on her lap to pat-a-cake, she would not introduce waving good-bye in the same play session.

As was stated earlier, any ex-perience that taxes the baby's emerging understanding of how the world works is a challenge. Problems to solve, or challenges, permeate every aspect of the baby's daily experience. Below are a few examples of the challenges that occur naturally in a rich environment.

(1) Learning to let go of objects, to drop them (at two or three months).

(2) Struggling to get the eyes to follow what the hands are doing (at three or four months).

(3) Trying to reach for an object that is just out of reach, to sit up, to crawl, to walk, to climb.

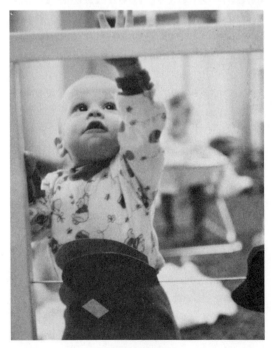

(4) Trying to achieve a certain arrangement of physical objects—for instance, stacking one block on top of another or putting a smaller can inside a larger one.

(5) Finding a ball that is not located where you expected it to be.

(6) Learning to tolerate mother's leaving without getting upset.

(7) Trying to match a word (spoken by an adult) with the object that it goes with.

Each of these situations, and many more like them, when presented at the right time to a responsive baby and with appropriate support, increases the baby's repertoire of skills and the pleasure of tackling new experiences.

Many social challenges involve encouraging the baby to communicate. A growing experience is set up each time a caregiver creates a situation that requires problem solving and communication, any kind of initiative on the baby's part. Opportunities to do this are numerous, but it takes a sensitive caregiver to see them and to be willing to take the extra time and effort to carry them out. The following example depicts this kind of caregiving.

A twelve-month-old is fussing, and the caregiver knows that this means she wants her bottle, which is sitting in the middle of the table, out of reach. The easiest thing for the caregiver to do is get the bottle and give it to her. Instead, she asks, "Dena, do you want your bottle?" She waits for Dena to respond by looking to the usual location. When she does, the caregiver moves the bottle to the edge of the table, giving Dena the opportunity to reach up and get it for herself.

As we have said, challenges exist in abundance in all areas of the baby's experience. One general category includes any experience that violates the baby's expectations about an event. This occurs in interactions both with people and with objects. For example, many social games that adults and babies play involve repeating an activity, building up an expectancy, and then doing what is not expected (for instance, in peek-a-boo or hiding games). A caregiver tickles a baby's tummy several times, each time holding her hand playfully above so the baby can see it. The laughter from the baby typically increases when she shifts suddenly after several times to tickle a foot instead. In routines, the baby comes to expect things to happen in a certain way and has to cope with changes and

delays. Toys often violate expectations, especially when they break
and no longer operate the way they
used to.[7]

Having considered a number of
important general characteristics of
meaningful play, attention is now
directed to a discussion of social
play.

SOCIAL PLAY:
ADULT AND BABY TOGETHER

The importance of pleasurable
interactions with adults for babies
of any age has been mentioned
many times. The recent emphasis
on infant education and early cognitive stimulation has resulted in
increased attention to toys and their
"educational value." This trend has
worked in a positive way to encourage people to think more about the
quality of experience for babies.
There is some concern, however,
that this emphasis on play materials has led to a de-emphasis of the
importance of social interactions
between infant and adult. **Toys
cannot be a substitute for being
with people.**

Social interaction with an
adult has many benefits for the infant. The baby undoubtedly is
learning that he or she is special
when the caregiver is devoting her
attention to him or her. The infant is
learning to trust people, and is
building a positive attitude toward
being with them. Participating actively in pleasant interactions with
adults also helps the baby to develop social competencies, to learn
appropriate ways of getting attention—for instance, that a smile usually brings a smile in return—or,
more generally, that if you can
somehow communicate an interest
or a need, it will usually be responded to. Social mastery is just as
important as mastery of other developmental skills used with inanimate objects. A social situation
offers many opportunities for both
kinds of mastery.

In a group program caregivers
must have time to spend with individual babies, time when their attention does not need to be on several babies at once. Such times
occur during routines—feeding,
diapering, for instance—but additional one-to-one time should be
incorporated into the day, for this is
one of the best opportunities for
caregiver and baby to get to know
one another. If possible, there
should be occasions for the caregiver and baby to leave the room
together to play alone or go on an
excursion. Many babies need some
time away from the group. Caregivers do also! Getting out of the room
gives them both a change of scen-
ery. Further, some babies play better, or at least differently, when
they are away from the group, and
this time out offers the caregiver a
chance to get a better picture of the
baby's skills. One of the caregivers

in the Cornell program reported that the time she spent out of the room with one baby was her favorite time in the day. She enjoyed caregiving and was very competent, so it is not likely that she enjoyed being out of the room simply because that was easier than being in it!

There are several general guidelines for effective social interaction between adults and babies.

1. **Play involving adults and babies should be interactive or reciprocal.** This involves both people influencing each other, each at times initiating social contacts, and each responding to the social approaches of the other. Even in the first few weeks of life babies find faces and people among the most interesting objects in their environment, and they are typically very responsive to social approaches from adults. Fussy babies will often quiet when they are picked up. They become very still as they listen to someone singing or talking, and they smile and coo contentedly when touched and talked to. Early in life babies can also initiate social interactions, and caregivers should be tuned in to them and respond appropriately. Looking at the caregiver's face, following her visually around the room, smiling, reaching shakily for her finger—these are some of the baby's first social behaviors, which result very often in social reactions from the adult. As babies get older, their social initiations as well as responses become more obvious, but they are no less important. Any positive social initiation by a baby merits a reaction. It is never appropriate to ignore intentionally an overture of this kind from a baby, for example, by refusing a block being offered, ignoring a smile or a wave, or not answering a babble.

In order for an interaction to involve both the caregiver and the infant actively, the caregiver must be careful not to overwhelm the baby with her own activities. Rather, she creates opportunities for the baby to respond and encourages his or her responses by showing pleasure or by responding in turn. For example, a caregiver helping a baby stand up from a sitting position does not repeatedly pull the baby up to standing by the arms and sit him or her down again. The caregiver might do this a few times, then wait to feel the baby pushing with one or both legs, or trying to pull himself or herself up by holding on to the caregiver. Playing is not something done *to* babies, it is done *with* them.

2. **Caregivers must be sensitive to cues the baby is giving them and adapt the play accordingly.** The most valid clue that an activity is successful is the baby's response.

If the baby is happy and interested, it will show. If the baby is not interested, the caregiver is unlikely to enjoy the play and may thus discourage the baby from interacting further with her or the toys. She must note such signs of interest as cooing, reaching, smiling, and signs of disinterest such as turning away or fretting, and she must know how to judge these reactions in individual babies. For example, not every baby will squeal and laugh gleefully when the caregiver puts a diaper over his or her face for a game of peek-a-boo. Some will, but others, who may be enjoying the game very much, may only smile slightly. One good cue is whether the baby, if he or she has the ability, helps in the play. That is, a baby who is smiling very little but is working hard to get the

diaper back over his face after he pulls it off obviously wants to continue the game.

Generally speaking, caregivers should pursue an activity only if the baby seems to be enjoying it. Of course, she may persist for a short time if she thinks that the baby is not really paying attention or giving the activity a chance, but when the baby has tried it and still shows minimal interest, she will stop and turn to something else.

The baby's general mood and behavior will suggest the most appropriate kind of play. A fussy baby beginning to get tired or a baby at loose ends near going-home time might perhaps enjoy a close, quiet time with the caregiver, learning to play pat-a-cake, looking at a book, singing, or talking. Some toys or activities could be saved especially for times like these. It was mentioned earlier that babies sometimes become "obsessed" with an activity and should be given the freedom to pursue it. Caregivers, perceiving these interests, should provide appropriate activities. For example, a baby who is mouthing everything should not be given a lot of play materials that are not suitable for chewing, for that would be more frustrating than fun. Stackers need objects that stack, mouthers need toys to chew on, climbers need equipment for climbing.

Another aspect of adaptability is that the caregiver should be able to drop her own previous plans and expand on variations in the activity that the baby initiates. For example: a caregiver has a nine-month-old in her lap and is helping him learn to pat-a-cake. He claps his hands together enthusiastically for the first two lines of the verse, but instead of "rolling it and patting it," he begins to pat his cheeks, then his knees. A baby-centered caregiver will see this as an initiation, a creative variation by the baby, and will drop "pat-a-cake" at least temporarily and begin imitating the baby, perhaps expanding on his variation by saying cheeks and head and hands as he touches them. Caregivers must guard against getting so wrapped up in an activity they have initiated that they forget the baby! For instance, if a caregiver is rocking a baby and singing to him, and

he begins to coo, she might stop singing to respond to his vocalizations.

Play is often used as a form of distraction to quiet a fussy baby. Some babies need only to have their attention diverted when they are distressed, while others need to be soothed before they can get involved in play. If a caregiver introduces an activity and the baby continues to be fussy, she may find another approach more helpful.

3. **Interactions between adults and babies should involve many different ways of communicating.** These ways include looking, talking, moving, holding, rocking, touching, singing, smiling, laughing. Especially with younger babies, the interaction should include a lot of close physical contact. Babies at any age need physical closeness, but very often older babies are too "busy" to spend long periods of time being held and rocked. Young babies are more likely to enjoy it. In general, it can be said that the appropriateness of certain kinds of interactions will depend on the developmental status and style of the baby.

4. **Language plays an important role in social interaction with babies at any age.** Just as the human face is one of the most interesting objects for even a very young baby to react to, so does the human voice play a large role from the begin-

ning. Very young babies enjoy being talked to and sung to long before they can understand words, and they learn much from this. Caregivers should therefore spend a good bit of time talking to babies and responding verbally to their early vocalizations. Conversing with a very young baby may feel slightly artificial in the beginning, but this feeling is soon replaced by pleasure at the baby's positive response to the talking. Our recommendation is that caregivers talk with even very young infants in a sensible and natural way, avoiding "talking down" or using an excessively simplified kind of "baby talk." Thus, the infant is exposed from an early age to the ordinary language of adults, and at the same time the caregiver will not need to change her language drastically as the baby gets older. Of course, this should not suggest that playful imitation of babies' babbling and cooing sounds should be discouraged. On the contrary, these early playful encounters serve a useful purpose in encouraging vocalization and social responses.

Using children's books is a particularly pleasurable way to combine talking and other ways of communicating with a baby. A caregiver who holds a six-month-old on her lap and talks about the pictures in the book they are "reading" together is doing many good things at once: she is holding the baby, giving him or her individual attention, creating interest in the bright colors and shapes in the book, and talking to the baby.

With babies in the first year of life, language is used in four ways: (1) as an interesting and unique source of stimulation, (2) as a means of soothing and comforting, (3) as a way of communicating feelings, and (4) as a tool for giving and receiving information. The first three uses of language apply from the first few weeks of life on. Further, children begin to understand language before they begin to use words and talk themselves. Therefore, the use of language as a tool for giving and getting information becomes a consideration for caregivers when babies are around six months of age, when it becomes very important that caregivers label familiar objects and activities in their natural conversations. By the time babies are around a year of age, they have begun to associate names with familiar objects. To encourage this learning, numerous games can be played with caregivers asking the baby to find an object named. Sometimes babies will respond by looking in the right direction only, making no attempt to point to or approach the object. Caregivers should note this visual response, too, and praise it warmly.

Babies will be encouraged to communicate verbally if their early attempts are responded to. Quite often the babies' early words bear little resemblance to standard English. It is frequently a real challenge for caregivers to discern what the baby means by a particular conglomeration of sounds, but the discovery that the baby is using a ''word'' consistently and ''correctly'' makes the caregiver's effort worthwhile.

5. **Interactions should occur naturally.** Very simply, the implication of this guideline is that babies benefit from being with adults who show a natural range of affect and emotions. Babies undoubtedly learn emotions partially by imitation. Caregivers are not entertainers, and should not be expected to be jolly all the time. While they may need to modify their negative feelings more than their positive ones, it is not realistic to expect them to be always happily receptive to babies' overtures, and it is important that older babies learn to sense when others may be displeased or impatient with them and the circumstances under which this occurs (see ''The Beginnings of Self-Control,'' Chapter 6).

Social situations also play a very important role in facilitating the learning of a variety of problem-solving skills involving inanimate objects. Toys and materials can be seen as tools to set up pleasurable interactions between adults and babies. The value of an adult and baby having fun together with a sorting box, for example, lies partially in what the baby is learning about matching shapes and putting things in, and partially in what is being learned about other people and oneself.

In addition to the five guidelines just discussed, there are other considerations that apply primarily, though not exclusively, to a situation where a caregiver and baby are playing together with a toy or any kind of play material.

6. **Adults can help babies learn new ways of mastery.** This principle is tied closely to the earlier discussion of challenges. New ways of mastery, finding the solution to a problem, discovering a different way of doing something familiar are often the result of appropriate challenges provided for babies either in materials or in demands for social and communication skills. From a knowledge of the baby—his or her developmental level, competencies, and style—the caregiver will know the level of challenge to which the baby will respond best. The caregiver may decide, for example, that making a particular situation easier will encourage a baby to work harder. If a four-month-old, lying on his stomach, is reaching out for a colored block that is about six inches beyond his reach, the sensitive caregiver will move it closer to him

so that he will have a better chance of grasping it. In the same situation with an eight-month-old, she would be less likely to move it closer if the baby was beginning to show an interest in crawling. There are, of course, numerous ways for the caregiver to give help, but she should give only enough help to still maintain the baby's efforts and interest, and show her approval, for in as much as possible, the *baby* should master the situation, not baby and caregiver together. For instance, in helping a baby to learn that pulling a string attached to a toy will bring it closer, she would pull it only part way, encouraging the baby to do the rest.

Caregivers can also demonstrate ways of mastery and thus capitalize on babies' ability to learn through imitation. Demonstrations should not be overdone, however, for the object is to encourage the baby to be curious, to explore and discover the world himself or herself, rather than being shown what to do by an adult. The caregiver can suggest variations at an appropriate time when interest is waning. For example, she might show an eleven-month-old that the blocks he has been mouthing and hitting together will stack nicely, or that they can be put inside a coffee can and dumped out again.

The caregiver's reaction to a baby's activities can be either encouraging or discouraging. Praise should be used appropriately, not as a standard reaction to everything the baby does. By showing pleasure in a baby's efforts and accomplishments, the caregiver is encouraging play. In many situations her enthusiasm and enjoyment may be much more valuable than any specific help she could offer. A baby can detect the approving tone in a caregiver's voice long before understanding what "good" means.

In a very direct way, a caregiver helps babies to learn new skills by setting up appropriate situations and participating in them. For instance, she can do more than just assume that a three-month-old baby has the opportunity to follow moving objects. When the infant is receptive, the caregiver may want to play with him or her occasionally by holding a brightly colored ball in

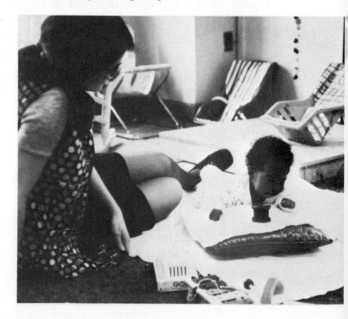

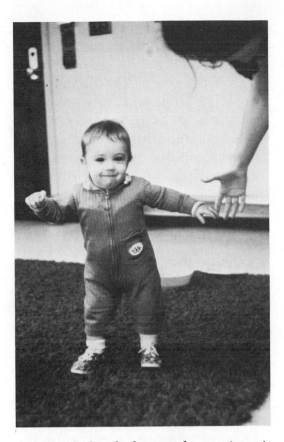

nearby and watching. For instance, a styrofoam egg carton has an interesting shape and feel, and blocks can be fitted into it nicely. However, it could be chewed, and a baby who is likely to try to eat it cannot be trusted with it alone.

7. **In presenting a new play material, a caregiver should let the baby discover it himself or herself and exploit it as he or she wishes for a time.** The caregiver's role is to *facilitate* the baby's interest and learning, to foster curiosity and exploration, *not to direct* the activities. Therefore, the infant is given the opportunity to discover and explore first, and then the caregiver may show the baby other ways to play. This does not mean that the caregiver is involved in the baby's play with a toy only when the baby is not interested by himself or herself—the caregiver may be right there, tuned in to what is being done, showing pleasure and

front of the baby and moving it slowly back and forth, up and down, and in an arc, or by moving around the crib so the baby can follow her visually. A baby will typically stay with an activity longer when the caregiver is there, so her presence may be encouraging the baby to work hard.

Emphasis is placed in this chapter on babies making choices in play, having freedom to explore and pursue their interests. Another role of the caregiver in playing with a baby is a supervisory one—that is, some toys which would not be safe for a baby to play with alone can be used effectively when a caregiver is responding while the baby does most of the work. Children should have the fun of discovering what can happen when they act on their world—that a mobile dances to its own music when hit, that pulling a string attached to a truck will bring it nearer, that moving one's body a little bit in order to get a block that is just out of reach is hard work but worth it. Figuring things out for oneself, solving problems, working long and hard to accomplish a goal is rewarding, even for babies. (This emphasis on the importance of self-discovery does not, of course, imply that a caregiver should let a baby play for a long time with a closed jack-in-the-box without demonstrating how to open it!)

8. **Caregivers should be tuned in to variations in play initiated by the baby and follow them up.** The caregiver must get rid of any preconceived ideas she has about the "correct" way to play with a particular toy. Letting the baby use his or her own curiosity and initiative in exploring is a far more valuable experience than having it done exactly as the instructions on the box state. Sensitive caregivers say "no" very rarely in play, except when the baby might possibly do some physical harm to himself, herself, or someone else. One of the major goals of play in the first year is to nourish a curious, assertive approach to the world. To do this, the baby must be allowed freedom to explore in a secure setting.

9. **Caregivers should encourage babies to persist, to work hard in trying to achieve reasonable goals.** As mentioned earlier, appropriate challenges are those activities which are difficult for a baby at a certain point in his or her development to complete successfully, but are *possible*. The caregiver's role is to provide such challenges and to encourage the baby to work hard at them. She should intervene with help before the baby gets upset and quits, but not before he or she has "wrestled" with the problem. Knowing what that point is comes as the result of attentively watching each baby play over a period of time. Often it is difficult for a conscientious caregiver to understand that leaving a baby alone can be good caregiving, but babies learn from tackling a problem and working hard at it, from trying to figure things out for themselves.

Consider, for example, a twelve-month-old who has managed to climb, with some effort, into the lower shelf of a cabinet which has been emptied just for that purpose. He is pleased with himself, but the quarters are cramped, and he has some trouble turning his body around in the small space in order to climb out. He whimpers. The caregiver, seeing that he is making progress, encourages him by saying, "That's it, Robert—you're doing a good job." She does not come over immediately and turn him around or take him out. He works again, and when he finally gets out, the caregiver lets him know clearly by her tone and words that he has just worked very well in completing a hard job. She has encouraged him to finish, and thus let him discover that he is a competent person who can solve problems on his own. Because of their relationship, he also knows that if the situation had been more difficult, more frustrating, he could have counted on her to help him out of it.

Giving just the right kind of help in just the right amount at the right time is superlative caregiving—and is a goal to be worked toward constantly. For one baby, moving a toy that he is trying to reach just a bit closer gives him the incentive to keep working, while for another baby the caregiver might decide to put the toy well within reach this time, let the baby hold it for a while, and then later move it further away. When the caregiver intervenes in such situations, she typically makes the activity easier, such as by giving a boost to a baby trying to crawl into a rocking chair, or demonstrating an easier way to climb by placing one knee up on the chair and showing the baby how to hold on with both hands. A twelve-month-old frantically trying to put a square block through a small round hole in the sorting box might be shown either the square hole and how the block goes through it easily, or, if the caregiver thinks it more appropriate for the child's developmental level, she may show him or her how to lift the lid and drop any block in easily.

Caregivers need to remember that babies may have valid reasons for stopping an activity—for instance, they may be tired of it, or the activity may be too difficult for them. There is nothing sacred about finishing an activity, so the caregiver should not persist in trying to regain the baby's interest if there are signs that he or she is no longer interested. Caregivers should not be overzealous in providing challenges and encouraging persistence; as has been said, it is also valuable for babies to practice skills they have already mastered, to do easy and familiar activities.

10. **Each baby has an individual style of playing, and the sensitive caregiver adapts her style to each baby.** Some babies need no introduction to toys, for they move right in, begin to explore, and get very involved by themselves. The world is there to be touched, tasted, explored, and exploited. Other babies, more cautious, may need more support from an adult and will benefit from being shown various possibilities for play. These

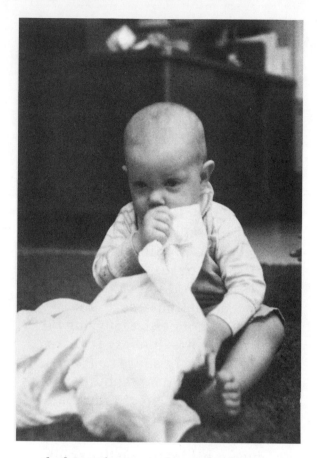

relatively little guidance in his or her play—the caregiver's role may be primarily sitting with the baby, talking and responding about the activity, reacting, but not distracting the baby. A baby with a more passive approach requires a more active role by the caregiver. She has to demonstrate possibilities, set up attractive play situations to involve him or her, and choose activities that will not be frustrating but rather very reinforcing for the baby. She must be relaxed in playing, and very careful to stop or change activities when the baby indicates that he or she is no longer interested.

PLAY MATERIALS

In the beginning of the chapter it was mentioned that the caregiver's role in babies' play is a double one: She is an interactor who participates directly in play with babies; and secondly, she arranges an ecology or physical setting that can either facilitate or impede play. This section is concerned with the second function.

The guidelines relating to the setting in which babies play and the materials they play with overlap considerably those discussed in the preceding sections on social play. The setting and the materials used influence significantly the kinds of social situations that arise. Play

babies frequently use their eyes without their hands to explore, even when they are older. These two groups can be termed the *actors* and the *watchers*. Some babies seem interested in and adept at learning by watching other babies or adults, while others need to *do* themselves, to *act,* in order to master. Both ways of learning are good, and respect for these individual differences supercedes any goal of having all babies become very active explorers.

The best way to know how to play with babies is to watch them. The more active explorer may need materials should be chosen carefully, for babies do not learn primarily by being given information verbally, but by watching and interacting.

The setting in which play happens is as important as the play materials themselves, since the arrangement and size of the play room, the caregiver's activities, and the way routines are carried out affect the babies' opportunities for play. Other sections of the book treat these topics more thoroughly. A safe, secure, comfortable setting, where babies are free to choose and explore and experiment, is necessary before it is appropriate to be concerned about play materials. It should be noted that the term *play*

materials refers not only to commercially made toys, but to materials found in the home that are safe and interesting for babies to play with. An empty box, a pot with a lid, a coffee can, and plastic refrigerator containers are ready-made creative play materials. Such "toys" also have the advantage of being familiar objects used by adults in the real world.[8] Appendix C offers suggestions for common objects that can be easily converted into interesting play materials.

The following guidelines apply to the selection of play materials and their use by babies alone or by babies with caregivers.

1. **Toys should encourage action.** Good play materials are not designed simply to entertain. To help babies learn, toys must elicit their active involvement. There are many entertaining toys on the market that demand very little of their users in the way of participation. For example, a current popular toy is a music box television with moving pictures. The dial that must be turned to wind the toy cannot be turned by a one-year-old child. Even very young babies are interested in the toy, for they enjoy looking at the moving pictures and listening to it, but for babies over six or seven months, it would be a better toy if they could operate it themselves.

2. **Play materials should respond to the baby's actions.** By doing something with an object, a baby should be able to bring about some kind of outcome that he or she can perceive. This kind of responsiveness in toys helps older babies to learn something about cause and effect relationships, which leads to mastery. The ability to control parts of one's world is something babies can begin to appreciate at a very early age. By the time the baby is able to use his or her hands to interact with the world and act on it to bring about changes, he or she has had experience in eliciting responses from people—someone usually comes when you cry, talks back if you talk. It is very important that caregivers consider the developmental level of each baby and provide materials that will be responsive. For example, a caregiver would not hold up a one-inch block for a four-month-old to grasp, but rather an eight-inch brightly colored ball. In selecting rattles for a

58

three-month-old, she would reject a white rattle with a muffled sound in favor of one that was brighter and made a more noticeable sound. For a six-month-old she might hang within the child's reach a box with a handle on a string which, when pulled, made music.

3. **The responsiveness of toys and play materials should be natural rather than "gimmicky."** With the advent of increasingly automated and electronically operated toys, cribs, playpens, and other equipment, it is possible to arrange a baby's world so that almost any action on the child's part will produce some kind of interesting external change—for example, a three-month-old's leg kicking can be made to turn on a colored light, start some music, or bring into view some plastic birds in a crib mobile overhead. We see no advantage, however, in providing infants with experiences of this kind. On the other hand, there is much advantage to be gained by giving the infant opportunities to produce changes in the environment by actions which can plausibly produce such outcomes in real life situations. For example, shaking or banging objects often produces interesting noises; turning an object over and over and inspecting it gives many different views of the surface; squeezing a soft object may produce interesting changes in its shape, as well as a funny squeak; dropping a block through a small hole so that it disappears and then waiting for it to reappear at the end of a chute can be an amusing game. These are illustrations of play materials which are responsive in a *natural* way to the child's actions and manipulations.

4. **A quality program includes both toys that encourage social interaction and those that can be used by a baby alone.** Since babies need to have some time alone, the room should be set up so that babies can spend some time safely and

constructively on their own. This again implies consideration of safety in room set up, the provision of a variety of age-appropriate toys, and sufficient physical space that babies have the freedom to pursue an activity alone—that is, with some protection from interruption by other babies. While all toys should not require the participation of another baby or adult, some toys should be around just for that purpose.

5. **Toys should be chosen and placed to give babies choices as they pursue their own interests, but with the aim of channeling their efforts to using emerging skills.** Caregivers encourage babies to choose their own toys, for instance by placing them on a shelf that is accessible even to crawling babies, but they may want to direct babies' efforts toward using new skills by the kinds of toys that are made available. An example given earlier in a slightly different context applies here: Stackers need objects to stack, mouthers should have a choice of objects that are safe to chew on, climbers need climbing equipment. Providing appropriate challenges for babies to work on can be facilitated by the kinds of toys in the setting. For example, a baby who has just learned to place a round piece in a form board should have access to that material as well as to the more difficult form boards

requiring placing squares or triangles.

The baby's involvement and enjoyment are a good gauge of the value of an experience. However, it is not enough to say that babies should be left with an activity as long as they are content. The four-month-old, mentioned earlier, who might be content to spend most of the time looking at complex visual patterns needs also to be attracted to an activity that demands the use of his hands.

One way to encourage babies' emerging interests is to provide reasonable alternatives to certain

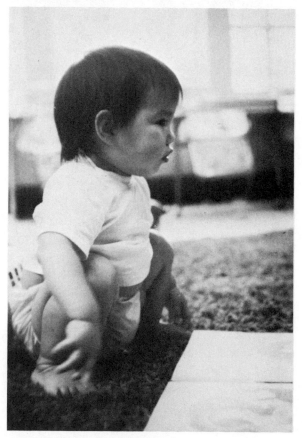

60

activities. For instance, a baby who has been looking at a book with a caregiver may show an interest in looking at and handling the book alone. Most books are not sturdy enough typically to withstand being "read" alone by babies, but an old wallpaper catalogue is ideal for that purpose.

6. **Play materials should be versatile—that is, they should lend themselves to a variety of uses.** In setting up a program, caregivers would want to select a variety of kinds of toys with a range of uses. At the same time, in considering individual toys, those toys are best which allow for a number of uses. The obvious example of this is a set of small colored wooden blocks. These can be looked at, reached for, banged together, mouthed, tossed, stacked, hidden, put in containers, dropped. One could contrast the number of uses for a set of blocks by a group of babies in the first year with that for the music box television mentioned earlier.

Around twelve months of age, babies become very interested in putting objects inside containers, so a quality program would offer many opportunities for this. Also around the same age, babies are beginning to be able to judge many similarities and differences. A wise caregiver, considering both of these interests, might use two coffee cans, some large and small blocks, and encourage the baby to separate the big ones and the little ones. This gives the baby the opportunity to use these emerging skills, an opportunity which he or she might miss if given only a single can filled with a random set of blocks. Toys like these elicit creativity and involvement on the baby's part rather than restricting activity.

Babies have an ever-increasing repertoire of things they can do with and to objects. Very early they mostly look, then can bat at objects, then reach toward them shakily, then grasp with both hands; eventually they can sit up, pass objects from hand to hand, hold two objects at once, combine two objects in play, move around, grasp smaller objects, and manipulate objects easily. The list grows and grows. Play materials should exploit all the abilities a baby has at a particular developmental level. For example, a mobile out of reach is not an appropriate toy for a four-month-old, who is beginning to reach actively for objects.

7. **Play materials should provide experience in a variety of modalities.** Diversity in the kinds of feedback a toy provides is important. For instance, a mobile that makes music when the figures move is giving more kinds of feedback than a silent one. A texture book offers a baby something interesting to touch and feel as well as to look at. A rattle of clear plastic, so that the baby can see where the noise comes from, may be more interesting than an opaque one.

* * *

In purchasing toys for a group program for babies, there are several additional considerations that are worth mentioning.

Safety—Are there detachable parts that could be swallowed? Is it breakable, so that there would be wooden splinters or sharp pieces of plastic? Is the paint nontoxic? Are there points that might be stuck in the eyes or nose? Is it safe for use alone, or does it require supervision with some babies? For instance, a plastic rattle is safe in the hands of a three-month-old, but a nine-month-old who is teething might bite on it vigorously enough to break it.

Attractiveness—It is often difficult for an adult to specify what makes a toy attractive to a baby. A toy that is bright and colorful is much more likely to attract interest initially. However, adults should never try to prejudge whether or not a baby will like a certain play material, but should give him or her the opportunity to try it and watch the interaction. A baby's initial disinterest or negative reaction to a toy should not be the final judgment. The caregiver may want to put it away and offer it again later. For example, some younger babies may be frightened by a toy that makes a loud or sudden noise, like a jack-in-the-box. A few months later, the same toy may be of great interest.

Durability—Is the toy made to withstand rough treatment over a period of time? A toy that might last for several months when used by one child may succumb after only a few days as a favorite toy of a group of babies.

Appropriateness for babies of different ages—Especially if budgets are limited, one would want to consider how wide an age range of infants would find the toy interesting. For instance, a sorting box could be used by an older baby for sorting, but the blocks could also be mouthed, grasped, reached for, and banged by younger babies. Toys carefully chosen can be used in simple and more complex ways by babies at different ages.

If a toy is fun—that is, if babies enjoy playing with it—then it is not necessary to worry too much about its educational value. At the same time, it is an interesting exercise to step back and consider a toy in

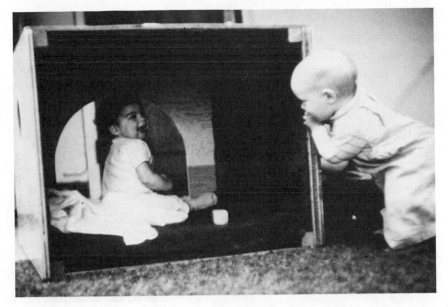

terms of what a baby could learn from it. The results may be surprising and very useful in guiding the selection of play materials.

INTERACTION OF BABIES WITH BABIES

Babies are interested in each other very early in life.[9] Before they can sit up or move around at all, they enjoy looking at other babies as they lie or sit in infant seats nearby. As babies become mobile, their curiosity leads to many pleasant and some unpleasant interactions with other babies as they explore them, sometimes very vigorously. Before the first birthday, though, many babies will begin to interact in a positive social way with other babies. The interaction

is not usually sustained for a long time, but it is not unusual to see a baby trying to get another baby to chase her or be chased by him, two babies laughing together over their own peek-a-boo game, or taking turns putting objects in a container. Observing the emergence of these early social behaviors is one of the most exciting privileges a caregiver has. A caregiver sensitive to the babies' interest in each other can help them learn to enjoy one another by setting up and participating in play situations involving two or more babies.

Some babies seem much more interested than others of the same age in playing with other babies. Whereas with older children the caregiver's goal might be generally to promote interaction with other children, at this age the baby's preference should be respected. While encouraging play with other babies for some infants, the caregiver also needs to protect them from each other when they begin to interact in overly vigorous or rough ways. She wants to ensure that the interactions that babies have with each other are mostly pleasurable.

Babies can begin to learn appropriate ways of interacting with each other long before their first birthday. They learn largely by example and with consistent guidance on the part of the caregiver. From brief encounters older babies may begin to get a sense of satisfaction from playing with someone else. The caregiver can also provide guidance by redirecting inappropriate behavior. For example, a baby starting to pull the hair of another baby has his or her hand taken gently by the caregiver and placed gently (open!) on the baby's head and moved across it as the caregiver talks about it. Praise for gentleness and appropriate interactions also helps. Constant use of verbal prohibitions, however, does little good.

Caregivers must be very watchful when babies begin to play together, but they should not always hover over them, for the presence and attention of a caregiver often impedes rather than facilitates play with another baby. Sometimes babies can work out disagreements over property rights, for instance, and should be given the opportuni-

ty to do so. At the same time, however, a baby involved in an activity alone should be able to work at it without interruption as long as he or she wants to and may need a caregiver's assistance in doing this.

The caregiver's role, then, is to give babies the opportunity to interact, for instance by placing younger babies together on a blanket with some toys. When babies are older, she may become a referee, sometimes deciding to separate two babies or to provide an alternative toy for one of them. One type of social interaction which she will discourage is teasing, which happens surprisingly early (around ten to twelve months). A baby will succeed in taking a toy from another baby, but instead of going off to play with it, may seem to want to flaunt it in front of the other baby, who inevitably will decide to want it back, even if he or she gave the toy up rather willingly.

Having enough space and having the room set up so that babies can sometimes get away from the group is important. A small, cramped room where babies have no choice but to be close to each other most of the time is not conducive to pleasurable interactions. Having enough toys for everyone, with duplicates of favorites, will eliminate some unpleasant encounters.

In summary, most babies enjoy and learn from being with other babies, and a quality program provides opportunities for pleasurable interactions for those babies who are interested.

CONCLUSION

Many guidelines for providing good play experiences, with specific examples, have been discussed in the foregoing sections, with emphasis on the quality of the play experience. However, this discussion of play should not be taken to imply that the people and the physical environment should be "bombarding" the baby constantly with input. While the setting should be rich and exciting, it should, at the same time, provide a relaxed atmosphere with opportunities for quiet time, time alone, and time for "doing nothing." This is one of the

issues considered in the earlier discussion of the general principle that babies need protection from overstimulation and disorder (Principle 7, Chapter 1). This topic is also closely related to the previous discussion of the need for stability and predictability in the people and setting as a precondition to effective social interaction and active exploration. In the context of the present discussion of play, the question can be stated as "How much is too much?"[10]

It is true that in a group program for babies, caregivers must guard against having so much going on, so many things infants will respond to, that it distresses them or decreases their involvement in activities. It certainly can be said with great confidence that during all their waking time babies need to have available a choice of people and objects to interact with. Most people find it fairly easy to judge when a baby does not have enough to keep him or her interested in interacting with the environment. A baby who is bored will usually be irritable and restless. It is considerably more difficult to judge at what point a baby has too much stimulation—too many things to react to or interact with.

It is impossible to state categorically what the optimal quantity of input might be; usually the best guide for caregivers is the baby's own involvement and mood. If the baby is fussy or distractible, or interacts only very superficially with toys and people, it may mean that he or she is confronted with too many things, or too much of the same thing, to respond to. For example, if a young baby sitting on a blanket with a large number of toys around her picks each one up for a short time and then exchanges it for another without exploiting it, she may have too many choices. In the same way, if a baby is playing busily with a particular toy and a caregiver keeps offering him new ones before he has a chance to exploit the last one, he quickly may lose interest in them altogether, because they are more than he can handle. Similarly, a baby who shows great pleasure when held high in the air a few times may begin to fuss if this is kept up too long.

While it is thought by many people that babies have the general capacity to "turn off," or to ignore stimuli, the possibility of overstimulation should still be of concern. A baby who frequently has to turn off noise and confusion is also very likely to turn off meaningful learning experiences as well. Overstimulation may be defined differently for each baby. Young babies, for instance, may be startled and upset by loud or unexpected noises that an older baby would find entertaining. Some babies are very adept at filtering out irrelevant stimuli and pursuing their own activities, while others are more apt to notice everything and try to respond to it. The latter group of babies need more protection, more quiet time, for they tend to be excitable and become very frustrated when their attempts at responding to everything and everybody are thwarted. Knowing each baby's style will affect the way a sensitive caregiver interacts with them. A day care program should provide daily opportunities for babies to be by themselves, to spend some time doing whatever they want to, thus somewhat controlling the amount of stimulation they prefer.

Earlier in the chapter, in the discussion of the need for a balance of sameness and variety (Principle 4, Chapter 1), it was mentioned that older babies are freer to create their own balance of sameness and variety than are younger babies. In the same way, mobile babies have more control over the kind and amount of input they are exposed to than do younger babies. It seems especially easy for caregivers to "overload" younger babies. They may assume, for example, that if their main way of exploring is through looking, then the more things they have to look at, the better off they will be. This is not so, for the baby may be overwhelmed with too much to look at. Also, if too many birds and butterflies and bells and balls hanging over and around the baby's crib keep him or her from looking around the room, then the baby is not exploring the world in the most meaningful way.

In this chapter, major emphasis has been placed on adapting the social and physical environment to the babies' interests and to their developmental status. As previously mentioned (Chapter 3), there are a number of considerations that would lead to the recommendation that programs can be planned best if babies less than twelve to fifteen months old are cared for, at least part of the time, separately from older babies. It was the experience in the Cornell program that the needs of babies, especially regarding play, change rather markedly around the end of the first year. Although our program involved more experience with younger babies than with one- to two-year-old children, it was obvious that the general program set up for the older group would need to be very different in some ways from that which is optimal for infants under the age of one year or so, and as young as six to eight weeks. Of course, the basic guidelines and principles would be the same. Many of the important things babies are learning about in the first year of life can be learned from events which occur naturally in the environment—learning to differentiate shapes, colors, and sizes, learning that people and ob-

jects sometimes disappear and return again, that they look different from different vantage points, but are still the same people or objects, that adults are trustworthy and fun to be with, that some kinds of actions on the baby's part usually have an effect on people or objects, or that certain words are associated with particular objects and acts. The list is endless. These kinds of experience constitute the main content or focus of play and learning in the first year. That is why one of the core concepts of this book is that every experience is potentially a meaningful learning experience for the young baby. Of course, this general principle continues to be valid not only in the second year of life, but in subsequent years as well.

After the end of the first year of life, approximately, exploiting naturally occuring events in an interesting, secure, and responsive setting that encourages exploration is still necessary, but this is no longer sufficient to ensure optimal play and learning experiences.

The kinds of activities one-year-olds are interested in, the skills they are developing, require more one-to-one situations with adults than when they were younger. It is still important to take advantage of opportunities for learning that occur naturally, but at the same time having some more structured, preplanned learning activities seems appropriate with older babies. For instance, when a caregiver and a six-month-old baby "read" a book together, the caregiver may tell the story, pointing and talking about the pictures. Eight months later, with the same book and the same baby, the caregiver might identify some of the most familiar objects pictured in the book and engage the baby in a simple game of matching pictures and objects. Again, it is difficult to provide for this kind of experience in a mixed-age program where, for instance, two caregivers are caring for eight children ranging from three or four months to fifteen months of age.

At around one year of age, babies begin to engage in much more intentional kinds of behavior—that is, they are more aware of what they want to accomplish, and they become much more concerned about completing something they set out to do. Their attention span lengthens and they tend to become very upset if their play is interrupted. Whereas at six to ten months a baby involved with a toy often will not mind if it is taken away by another baby, at one year of age he or she will. Older babies need the freedom to finish what they begin, to work on tasks uninterrupted by younger babies who cannot understand property rights. This freedom is difficult to provide in a program which includes babies

under and over a year playing together.

Younger babies often are less compliant than older ones. Although they are curious and motivated to learn, their attention span is very short, they are distractible, and it may be difficult for an adult to keep them engaged in an activity for very long. At twelve to fifteen months babies become considerably more "teachable"—that is, they are beginning to have some understanding of language, to communicate themselves, and to begin to be able to follow simple directions.

Whatever the age of the baby, whatever the setting, perhaps the single most important point to be made about play is that it should be fun for everyone participating, caregivers as well as babies. Caregivers should view the babies' early play experiences as an opportunity to lay the foundation for an attitude that learning is fun (Principle 10, Chapter 1). There are five major ways in which babies learn that learning is fun: (1) by having their physical and social needs met consistently; (2) by having the opportunity to become involved in a variety of pleasurable learning activities; (3) by observing and imitating adults who enjoy learning and show their enjoyment in a way that babies can understand; (4) by receiving appropriate help and encouragement; (5) by being praised for accomplishments.

Play, as it has been considered here, represents far more than cognitive stimulation, educational toys, curriculum for development, or baby learning; but it includes elements of all of these. Essentially, it is *experience*—experience that lays a base for developing positive attitudes about the world of people and objects, as well as for understanding how the world works.

Chapter 5. Play and Learning—Notes

1. Our use of the term *play* in the present context is somewhat broader than one finds in most discussions of play in early childhood which tend to focus primarily on activities of toddlers and older children. On the other hand, while not referred to by everyone as play, the importance of the kinds of spontaneous, exploratory, pleasurable interactions between the infant and the immediate environment which we stress in this chapter has been recognized for some time, and is emphasized in many recent discussions of the infant as an active explorer and learner, such as those listed below.

Stone, L.J., and Church, J. *Childhood and Adolescence,* 3rd ed. New York: Random House, 1973.

This book contains a particularly good overview of behavior and development during the first fifteen months of life (Chapters 2 and 3) and during the toddler period, from fifteen months to two and one half years (Chapter 5).

Sutton-Smith, B. *Child Psychology.* New York: Appleton-Century-Crofts, 1973.

Chapters 5, 6, and 7 present a valuable summary of the behavior and development of infants, including a brief discussion of the role of play in intellectual and sensorimotor development (pp. 172-175).

The three articles below contain more specific treatments of play and learning as these relate to social and intellectual development early in life.

Murphy, L.B. "Spontaneous Ways of Learning in Young Children." *Children* 14 (1967):210-216.

Murphy, L.B. "Multiple Factors in Learning in the Day Care Center." *Childhood Education* 45 (1969):311-320.

Saunders, M.M. *The ABC's of Learning in Infancy.* Greensboro, N.C.: University of North Carolina Demonstration Project, 1971.

2. Weikart, D.P., and Lambie, D.Z. "Early Enrichment in Infants." In *Education of the Infant and Young Child*, edited by V.H. Denenberg. New York: Academic Press, 1970.

"The primary role of curriculum is (1) to focus the energy of the teacher on a systematic effort to help the individual child to learn, (2) to provide a rational and integrated base for deciding which activities to include and which to omit, and (3) to provide criteria for others to judge program effectiveness so that the teacher may be adequately supervised. The successful curriculum is one that permits this structuring of the teacher to guide her in the task of interaction with the theory she is applying on the one hand, and the actual behavior of the child, on the other . . . . The process of creating and the creative application of *a* curriculum, not the particular curriculum selected or developed, is what is essential to success . . . . In an almost romantic sense, the human involvement of concerned teachers and staff is the key element in program success . . . . In summary, . . . a curriculum is more important for the demands it places upon the project staff in terms of operation than for what it gives the child in terms of content." (pp. 89-90)

3. The following general references on typical patterns of growth and development in infancy are considered particularly valuable.

Church, J. *Three Babies: Biographies of Cognitive Development.* New York: Random House, 1966.

Life histories of three babies from birth to age two, based primarily on mothers' records with comments by a child psychologist.

Gesell, A., et al. *The First Five Years of Life.* New York: Harper, 1940.

Classical treatment of normal development in early childhood by a pioneering pediatrician-researcher in child development.

Stone, L.J., and Church, J. *Childhood and Adolescence* 3rd ed. New York: Random House, 1973.

Sutton-Smith, B. *Child Psychology.* New York: Appleton-Century-Crofts, 1973.

The reader is also referred to a rather detailed outline in Appendix B indicating approximate age of appearance of various developmental landmarks during the first two years of life. A briefer checklist of selected developmental landmarks for use by caregivers in informally noting progress of individual infants, as described in Chapter 8, is contained in Appendix F.

A useful overview of physical and biological growth in early childhood is contained in the following text.

Breckenridge, M.E., and Murphy, M.N. *Growth and Development of the Young*

Child. 8th ed. Philadelphia: W.B. Saunders, 1969.

See especially discussions of nutrition (Chapter 5); eating behavior and elimination (Chapter 6); activity, rest, and sleep (Chapter 7); and physical development (Chapter 9).

4. One of the best sources of information on development in the first year of life, with special emphasis on individual differences, is the following.

Brazelton, T.B. *Infants and Mothers.* New York: Delacorte Press, 1969.

5. Many suggestions of appropriate activities for babies of different ages are available. One of the best of these is in Chapter 4: "Activities for Infants," pp. 49-72, in *Day Care 2: Serving Infants.* (See Huntington et al., Introduction, note 3.)

6. Hunt, J. McV. *Intelligence and Experience.* New York: Ronald Press, 1961.

Hunt, J. McV. "The Epigenesis of Intrinsic Motivation and the Fostering of Early Cognitive Development." In *Current Research in Motivation*, edited by R.N. Haber. New York: Holt, Rinehart, & Winston, 1966. Also in Hunt, J. McV., *The Challenge of Incompetence and Poverty.* Urbana, Ill.: University of Illinois Press, 1969.

7. Pekarsky, D., Kagan, J., and Kearsley, R. *Manual for Infant Development.* No publisher given. Author's address: Dr. Jerome Kagan, Department of Social Relations, Harvard University, Cambridge, MA 02138.

The authors describe a program of activities based primarily on the importance of giving babies opportunities to work with contradictions of expectancies and variations in their daily activities.

8. Tronick, E., and Greenfield, P.M. *Infant Curriculum.* New York: Media Projects, 1973.

Upchurch, B. *Easy-to-do Toys and Activities for Infants and Toddlers*. Available from the Infant Care Project, The University of North Carolina at Greensboro, Greensboro, NC 27412.

9. Recent observations have led to the conclusion that the beginnings of social interaction between young children appear much earlier in life (that is, before the end of the first year) than was formerly thought to be the case. The following reports describing several studies of social interaction among infants in our day care nursery illustrate the point.

Durfee, J.T., and Lee, L.C. "Infant-Infant Interaction in a Day Care Setting." Paper presented at meetings of American Psychological Association, August 1973, Montreal, Canada. (Technical Report, Cornell Research Program in Early Development and Education. Ithaca, N.Y.: Cornell University, August 1973.)

Lee, L.C. "Social Encounters of Infants: the Beginnings of Popularity." Paper presented at meetings of the International Society for the Study of Behavioral Development, August 1973, Ann Arbor, Mi. (Technical Report, Cornell Research Program in Early Development and Education. Ithaca, N.Y.: Cornell University, August 1973.)

10. The problems of how best to define important aspects of stimulation in the infant's environment, and the determination of what levels and quality of stimulation can be considered optimal from the point of view of the infant's development, represent difficult issues which are currently very much under consideration and investigation. The following references provide some illustrations of recent studies involving systematic efforts to relate characteristics of the infants' early social and learning environment to various aspects of behavior and development.

Lewis, M., and Wilson, C.D. "Infant Development in Lower Class American Families." *Human Development* 15 (1972):112-127.

White, B.L., and Watts, J.C. *Experience and Environment*. Vol. 1 Englewood Cliffs, N.J.: Prentice-Hall, 1973.

Yarrow, L.J.; Rubinstein, J.L.; Pedersen, F.A.; and Jankowski, J.J. "Dimensions of Early Stimulation and Other Differential Effects on Infant Development." *Merrill-Palmer Quarterly* 18 (1972):205-218.

(The references contained in Introduction, note 1 also bear in part upon this general issue of stimulation and early development.)

Chapter 6

Helping Babies Adjust

Sensitive caregiving practices may be instrumental in influencing the skills a baby develops for expressing needs, getting attention from adults, and coping with frustrations. Two major areas of concern for people working with babies are coping effecitvely with distress and helping babies when they are ready to begin learning to guide their own behavior.

CRYING AND THE RELIEF OF DISTRESS

Understanding crying and distress in order to prevent their unnecessary occurrence and responding to them effectively are major concerns for anyone involved in caring for very young children.[1]* Caregivers in a quality day care program for babies should plan and carry out their daily activities with the aim of maximizing the babies' happiness and well-being and minimizing distress. There is relatively little agreement from research evidence on the significance of distress in babies and the best ways of reacting to it. Some studies suggest that responding to a baby's crying by picking the baby up, for instance, will result in an increase in crying over time, whereas if crying episodes are ignored, they will occur less often.[2] Other studies

*Footnotes for this chapter are located on pages 90-91.

support the alternative conclusion that responding quickly and appropriately to a baby's crying will reduce the frequency of later "fussing."[3] Practitioners—parents, caregivers, and other people who know babies well—also express diverse points of view about distress and its management.

The issue of coping with distress is complex, and the answer is undoubtedly not as clear and obvious as either of the two points of view suggests. It is clear that babies cry for many reasons, and the reasons change as babies get older, making this an area where sensitivity to individual differences is crucial. Caregivers have to work very hard to understand and anticipate distress in order to be even partially successful in reacting to it.[4]

The position taken here is that crying has meaning for the baby, no matter how young. Therefore, a person caring wisely for a baby *always* responds to crying by noticing it, considering its meaning and how one should react, and then reacting. This does not mean that a good caregiver always intervenes immediately when a baby cries. On the contrary, the caregiver may decide to wait for a time to give the baby an opportunity to quiet himself or herself. Also, a baby may cry, not because anything is wrong physically, but because he or she wants to be held close or played with. The caregiver respects these

needs and attends to them as she does needs for food, rest, or dry diapers.

The goal of a parent or caregiver obviously would not be to eliminate crying, for it is one of the baby's first and most important means of communicating with other people. It continues to be an effective way of communicating even after other ways are available. Crying is one of the earliest methods a baby has of exercising some control over the world (Principle 4, Chapter 1) and learning that people are responsive to his or her initiations. In responding to distress, therefore, the caregiver's goals should be to help the baby learn to trust other people, to know that his or her needs will be met, and that he or she will be responded to and given help and relief when it is needed. At the same time, she wants to encourage the baby to develop his or her own resources in

74

coping with some problems and unpleasant situations.

There are very wide individual differences among babies in the frequency, intensity, and causes of distress episodes.[5] While it can be said that all normal babies cry at some time and under some circumstances, there are not special cries for special occasions that are typical of all babies. It is true, however, that caregivers can become sensitized to the meaning of particular kinds and intensities of cries in individual babies—that is, whether they indicate hunger, pain, just mild fussiness, or a rather half-hearted attempt to protest, for instance. There are vast differences in the ways babies show distress, just as there is great variability in the way they show pleasure. For example, a fairly mild cry by one baby who seldom gets upset would be more a cause for concern than that same intensity of distress from a baby who is generally more irritable.

Babies also differ widely in their ability to quiet themselves when upset and therefore differ in the amount and kind of intervention they require from caregivers to be consoled when they are upset. Some young babies (less than three to four months old) become excited easily and are generally very "fussy." They may need much direct help in quieting themselves by being picked up, carried, and rocked, or, more indirectly, by being cared for in a serene, consistent, predictable setting. Caregivers should not worry about spoiling a young baby by responding quickly to crying, for this responsiveness and help will keep the infant from becoming uncontrollably upset now and will aid in the development of later skills for self-quieting. Some young babies can quiet themselves and should be given the opportunity to do this. The caregiver's response, in any case, depends on her understanding of the individual baby and her perception of the cause for the baby's distress. From the very beginning, the way the caregiver reacts to the baby's crying helps to build a relationship between them.

Causes of Distress

It is unrealistic to try to develop a complete list of causes of babies' crying and appropriate reactions by adults, for individual babies differ, and responses will depend both on the baby and the situation.[6] As babies become more active, more assertive, develop some understanding of language, and are more mobile, typical causes of distress change. The baby's increasing understanding of the social and physical worlds means that caregivers will react to distress differently when babies are older. There is typically more crying in the early months of life than later, and individual babies may show much more distress during certain periods in their development than others. Young babies may cry at times when there seems to be nothing wrong, and the lack of an apparent reason for distress makes it difficult for the caregiver to respond appropriately. As babies get older, the reasons for crying become more obvious. Instances of crying may become fewer in number but more intense and more sustained.

Some of the most common reasons for distress in very young babies (less than four or five months) are hunger, tiredness, wet or soiled diapers, pain (gas, teething, colic), other discomfort (clothing too tight, too warm, too cool, or an uncomfortable position), boredom (not enough going on around them to engage their interest), overstimulation (too much going on around them), a sudden change (for example, a loud noise, sudden loss of support, bright lights, being placed in a bath, being picked up abruptly). When crying occurs for one of these reasons, the baby should be responded to immediately and appropriately. A caregiver will sometimes have to respond to crying in a trial-and-error fashion, even with a baby she knows well. The caregiver's manner should be gentle and soothing in a deliberate way, for both she and the baby are likely to be feeling impatient with each other and themselves as the caregiver tries to relieve the baby's distress.

The paragraphs which follow contain a more detailed discussion of some of the major sources of distress in the first year of life in a group care setting.

Early frustrations. Around three or four months of age, new causes for distress arise. Not only do babies continue to cry for the same reasons as they did earlier, but as they become increasingly aware of the world around them, they seem to develop some awareness of their limited repertoire of skills. By this age, babies have the capacity to have modest goals in mind—visually following a moving object, for example. The discrepancy between what they want to do and what they are able to do becomes a source of frustration. A good example of the frustration which may lead to distress occurs in the early stages of reaching, when the baby's aim is not accurate and any efforts are fumbling. After several unsuccessful attempts to obtain an object, some babies seem to become very angry with themselves, and they may cry vigorously. In some of the babies in the Cornell program, it was observed that crying decreased as competencies increased. They became markedly less irritable when they began to creep or crawl well. As babies are able to do more, their frustration decreases, and they are happier. However, as babies become more mobile and take a more active, assertive, adventuresome approach to the world, they are certain to attempt to do many things they cannot do safely, to get themselves into problem situations. New frustrations and at least a few scratches and bumps are inevitable. By giving appropriate help, setting up an environment with as few hazards as possible, and reacting calmly but warmly when the baby gets upset, the adult can help the baby cope with limitations and at the same time learn a curious, investigating attitude toward the world.

Often babies become more impatient and easily upset during a time when they are attaining a new skill such as learning to walk or crawl. Their tolerance for frustration in most areas seems to drop as they direct their efforts toward developing new competencies. At these times, caregivers will want to be especially patient and helpful.

Babies also become distressed very early in life (around three to four months) when something enjoyable is terminated, such as when an adult withdraws attention or an interesting toy is removed. Crying sometimes indicates impatience, also, because needs are not being met fast enough. Learning patience and the realities about the way the world works can begin early. There needs to be a balance between helping the baby, making the situation easier to cope with or rescuing him or her from it, and letting the baby work things out for himself or herself. For example, a baby who is upset because a toy is out of reach and who cannot move to retrieve it should, of course, have it placed nearer. On the other hand, always accommodating a baby who does not like being put down after being held or who loudly protests the end of the applesauce at lunchtime may encourage excessive crying to get his or her own way or to get attention. A better response to this kind of crying is to distract the baby by engaging his or her attention with something else, by introducing a new toy, for example.

Distress at naptime. This is a

77

common occurrence with some babies ("Naptime," Chapter 7). Crying or less intense fussiness and whimpering may be the major cues a particular baby gives to indicate readiness for a nap. If the baby is not asleep when put down in the crib, he or she may cry, perhaps very loudly and intensely, before going to sleep. The infant may be irritated at having been taken away from the action and is tired—ample reasons for crying. If the caregiver is fairly certain that the baby is sleepy, she should leave the baby a while to try to work things out for himself or herself. Since one of the caregiver's goals is to help the baby learn to quiet himself or herself when upset, during this time the caregiver may want to go in, talk softly, and pat the baby. No set time for letting a baby cry at naptime before the caregiver intervenes can be designated, since this depends on the particular baby and the severity of the distress. The caregiver who knows a baby well can tell when the baby has reached the point where he or she will not be able to quiet himself or herself and go to sleep and therefore needs help. This might be as little as five minutes for one baby, or as long as fifteen to twenty minutes for another, particularly if the crying has been only intermittent.

When babies are around nine to twelve months old, the job of getting them to go to sleep may become easier, as the baby gets used to the routine and seems to accept napping or resting when tired. On the other hand, some babies at this age become less willing to miss what is going on in the room, and taking a nap may become rather difficult. Firm, affectionate, but consistent handling is especially necessary with babies who resist naptime if the sensitive caregiver is to ensure that the baby's needs for rest and sleep are adequately met. The caregiver should not see herself as losing or giving in when she has to help a baby get to sleep or take the baby out of the crib when he or she will not rest.

Unpleasant encounters between babies. As babies begin to move around, opportunities to interact with other babies increase. Many pleasurable play situations occur as babies discover each other. However, there will also be occasions when a baby causes another baby to become upset by exploring the child too roughly or taking a toy, for instance. The caregiver should view these occasions as opportunities to help both babies learn appropriate ways of interacting. Both babies in such a situation need support, sympathy, and redirection. Often separating them is the best solution. A duplicate toy might be introduced if sharing is a problem. The baby who is upset should be comforted, but the goal is to help both babies learn social skills. This might be a good time to

78

introduce a quiet activity, or to put a baby in a crib or playpen with toys for a time to become calm and renew energies.

Fearful responses to strangers. Sometime during the last half of the first year of life, many babies go through a period when they show negative reactions to strangers. This period should be respected, and the baby's feelings should be considered in the day care program. The caregivers should keep in mind the importance of having familiar persons care for the baby each day and provide some protection from exposure to large numbers of people the baby does not know. During the time when the baby is especially sensitive, the caregiver will want to be close, perhaps even holding him or her when a stranger is present. Unfamiliar people viewed from a caregiver's lap are less threatening than those seen from the floor. Of course, caregivers have to be careful not to be overprotective of babies who are distressed by strangers. If a caregiver runs to hold a baby protectively whenever a stranger enters, and encourages the stranger to stay at a distance from the baby or leave the room, the baby may be learning that new people are to be feared. Rather, through their relationship of trust, the caregiver is in an excellent position to help the baby begin to react positively to new people.[7]

Excessive confusion and change. Crying may both contribute to and reflect the atomosphere a baby is in. One cause of crying to be guarded against in group care centers relates to the overall atmosphere in the room—the noise level, the amount of activity, the calmness or confusion. As previously mentioned, some babies are much more capable than others of filtering out distractions and unnecessary sights and sounds impinging on them. More sensitive babies, who are less able to "turn off" distractions, become very upset when there are too many things happening around them. Planners of physical space and equipment as well as activities for babies must think about ensuring some calmness and serenity in the day. Babies who become upset because too much is going on need to be redirected to quieter, less exciting activities.

It is expected that babies may cry more than they usually do as they adjust to being in a new environment with new caregivers. This would also be true after a long time away from the day care program. After a few days, if a baby continues to show a great deal of distress and the caregivers cannot help, perhaps the parents should be consulted about what could be done to make the day care experience more pleasurable.[8]

Many common causes of distress have been discussed. However, there remain, even for the experienced caregiver, occasions when both the cause of distress and the appropriate response elude her completely, and she attributes it to the weather or some change of routine. Often the cause of general crankiness becomes obvious a few days later, when the baby develops a cold, ear infection, or some other illness. Here, too, parents and caregivers can be helpful to each other in looking for explanations.

Responding to Distress

There has been some discussion already of the ways caregivers may react to babies' distress. There are two additional, broader issues relevant to responding to distress: the appropriateness of giving and witholding attention in certain situations and how that affects the baby's use of distress to get attention; and secondly, the importance of giving babies some opportunities to learn to quiet themselves.

The importance of a great deal of individualized, personal attention for babies' development and general well-being is stressed throughout this book. While caregivers in a group setting will have many demands on their time and energy, they must guard against giving babies attention only when they cry. They should, rather, respond to positive social approaches and attempts to communicate by the babies. It was stated earlier in

this chapter that very young babies cannot be readily spoiled; that is, reacting quickly and perceptively to their distress will help them learn to use their own resources later. As babies get older, however, caregivers want to avoid communicating to them that the most effective way of getting attention is to cry. Many people disagree about when babies begin to use crying in a deliberate way to get something they want. Whether or not they use distress in this way before the end of the first year is debatable. It is clear, however, that a baby may learn very early in life that crying is a good way of attracting an adult's attention. If the baby is not sufficiently rewarded for more positive attempts to communicate (being picked up when holding out arms, being smiled at when smiling, for example), the baby may learn to rely primarily on distress to get attention (behavior many people would regard as characteristic of the spoiled baby). It is also true that some babies seem to want more attention than a caregiver can possibly give. On occasions when the caregiver feels that the needs of these babies have been met, including needs for individual attention in the form of social interaction and play, the caregiver might decide to ignore distress and see if its frequency decreases over time. With these babies, cooperation between parents and day care staff is impera-

80

tive if changes in the use of crying are to be made.

In thinking about when and how she should respond to distress, the caregiver must keep in mind the importance of both giving attention and support to the baby, as well as helping the baby develop the ability to quiet himself or herself. Babies need to learn to tolerate frustration and work out minor irritations on their own. It is difficult but wise for a caregiver to respond by doing and saying nothing when a baby is complaining over a small problem that she thinks the baby has the competence to work out on his own. Allowing the baby to do this is one way a caregiver provides appropriate challenges that lead babies to develop new competencies and skills.

The ability to quiet themselves when they are distressed is a dimension on which babies vary widely. Some babies, even if they become very distressed, seem to be able to calm themselves relatively easily after a period of being upset. They come out of these periods quickly and get involved easily in an activity. Other babies, when they get upset, seem to have to "cry themselves out," and their periods of distress become more intense and more sustained than those of the other group of babies unless they are helped by an adult to quiet themselves. For some babies, the caregiver may only need to say a

few comforting words at a distance, while with another baby in the same situation, she knows that she will have to go over, pick the baby up, and help him or her more actively to get over the crying.

In responding to distress, the caregiver looks first at the immediate situation for a cause. For example, maybe the baby is bored with the toys available, perhaps is in an uncomfortable position, may have been bothered by another baby, or perhaps has had a toy taken away. These are situations that can be corrected easily. If there is no obvious reason in the immediate situation for the crying, the caregiver will think about the baby's schedule and look for signs that he or she is sleepy, hungry, or needs a diaper change. If the fussiness is still unexplained, the caregiver thinks back to the mother's report and the day's observations to decide if the baby is teething or is reacting to medication or an injection or may be catching a cold or other infection. Then the caregiver may consider the possibility of a change in routine at home or in the nursery that could be upsetting, such as a parent or caregiver being away or a stranger's presence in the room.

Probably the most common (and most successful) responses to distress are functional ones— feeding a hungry baby, diapering a wet one, giving an interesting toy to

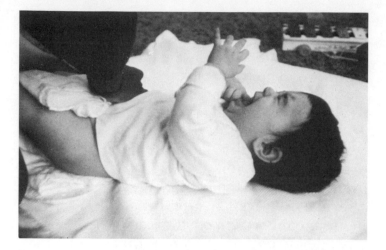

a baby who is bored. At other times the caregiver first has to calm the baby, to help stop the crying by holding, singing, or talking quietly to the baby. Sometimes the most soothing response for a baby who is in pain or ill or whose distress is of uncertain origin is holding him or her and rocking or walking, and singing or talking gently to the baby. Being comforted this way tells the baby he or she is cared about, and it may take his or her attention off the unhappiness for a time. Older babies can appreciate verbal reactions to distress better than can younger ones. Often a caregiver can quiet an older baby just by talking to the baby across the room, whereas younger babies need to be picked up or patted, as well. The caregiver's reaction should match the distress—that is, an occasion when a baby is really hurt or upset is not the time to give the baby the chance to quiet himself or herself.

In a group program, the *prevention* of distress should be as much a concern as coping with distress when it happens. A fussy baby contributes to an unpleasant, often tense atmosphere for other babies and caregivers, and can cause more distress. The best strategy for preventing distress and keeping it at a minimal level is to anticipate needs before they occur by knowing the babies' schedule and being alert to early signs of hunger, sleepiness, or irritability. Several other guidelines for minimizing distress relate to points made in other sections of the book.

1. Set up a safe, interesting environment that is not overly stimulating or too restricting.

2. Help babies learn to have pleasurable interactions with each other by protecting them from hurting each other as they begin to interact.

3. Provide many opportunities for success.

4. Give babies encouragement and help.

A wise general policy is for caregivers to minimize occasions likely to produce distress in the day-to-day operation of the program.

Many potentially distressful situations can be avoided by a sensitive caregiver who knows the baby's limitations and who does not see the baby's distress behavior as a deliberate effort to test her or make unreasonable demands. For instance, a baby who in the caregiver's judgment should not be hungry may get very upset if he or she has to stand by while another baby is being fed. A perceptive caregiver, rather than ignoring the problem or punishing the baby for being unreasonable, will help make the situation easier to tolerate. She might help the baby get interested in another activity or allow him or her to participate by eating a cracker or a piece of fruit while the other baby is being fed.

Most people who care for babies will agree that coping with distress is one of the most challenging issues they face, partially because of the obtrusiveness of crying. A baby's crying tends to affect negatively anyone who can hear it. A period of prolonged fussiness and crying will wear down even the most patient and understanding caregiver. At such times, having another caregiver take over for a while may be very helpful. Caregivers may have to be reminded that anger is always an inappropriate response to crying. Punishing a baby for crying will serve no constructive purpose and may be harmful. A caregiver working with an irritable baby who will not be quieted needs support and relief from other caregivers, for these times are perhaps the most difficult aspect of caregiving.

In general, having reasonable expectations and gearing the daily experiences to each baby's developmental level and style will minimize unnecessary distress and create a much happier setting for adults and babies. This theme was repeated many times in the previous chapter on play, which stressed the idea that very young children learn from dealing with an appropriate number of challenges or problems that are not immediately solvable. Coping with frustration and learning to tolerate delays and disappointments are challenges which sometimes lead to distress. The caregiver's role in reacting to babies' distress comes from a concern for making the baby's experience as pleasant as possible, but at the same time challenging the baby to develop his or her own resources.

THE BEGINNINGS OF SELF-CONTROL

It is surprising to some people that questions relating to setting limits and the beginnings of self-control, or discipline, are relevant considerations in working with groups of babies in day care. However, if one believes that babies' very early interactions with people and inanimate objects help them to learn about themselves and the world, then it follows that learning to guide one's own behavior in an adaptive way also begins to be important in infancy. The terms *discipline, setting limits, guidance of behavior* are all used to convey the rather basic idea of helping very young children begin to learn what are and are not considered appropriate behaviors, to be aware of cues from other people about the effects of their actions, and to direct their own behavior accordingly. In the broad sense of the term, then, discipline implies sensitive teaching which provides opportunities for learning.[9] As such, much of what is said in other chapters of this book relates to the topic.

The area of discipline is one where parents may have strong feelings about how their baby is handled. At the same time, it is one of the areas of early care where consistency between what is done at home and in the day care situation is most crucial to help the baby learn appropriate behaviors. Not only might there be wide disagreement about techniques of guidance, but the question of what are and are not appropriate behaviors varies greatly depending on cultural preferences, social group membership, as well as individual beliefs. Day care staff must be aware of this as an area where communication with parents is particulary necessary,

and compromises may have to be made.

There are several types of situations that come up in the first year of life requiring that babies begin to learn to direct their own behavior appropriately. First, being in a day care center offers babies very early opportunities to begin learning to get along with people their own age as well as with adults. Learning the give-and-take nature of interpersonal relationships, the pleasures as well as the frustrations of being with other people, is one of the most positive kinds of experiences that infants can have in a quality group care program. A second area involves helping babies learn to wait, to control impulses, to inhibit behaviors when the social situation requires it. A third impetus for setting limits for babies, trying to teach them to control their behavior, is a concern for safety—the babies' own safety, that of the people around them, and protection of material objects. These experiences will be positive only if caregivers understand the limitations of babies' abilities to guide their own behavior, and encourage them to be active, curious explorers of their environment rather than "well-behaved" babies.

Imposing restrictions, setting limits, helping babies learn controls must be balanced with the equivalent need of encouraging an active, curious, exploratory attitude toward the world. Too much emphasis on control, too many restrictions, will tend to discourage babies from exploring. **An adult interacting with a baby should not be concerned primarily with helping produce "good" babies who do not get into things, but, rather, active, curious explorers who do get into things.** Caregivers should not be overly concerned with teaching babies to behave, although older babies are ready to begin to learn some controls. It is important to guard against either extreme: excessive control, on the one hand, or allowing babies complete license, on the other. The discussion here has stressed minimal controls to encourage exploration in children under the age of one year. This is appropriate only in an environment where hazards to young children can be eliminated. There are, of course, some situations where, because there are more potential dangers in the environment, parents may want caregivers to place greater emphasis on learning obedience, which may be adaptive and necessary.

With younger babies (less than six to eight months), it is unrealistic to expect that they will readily learn to control their behavior or to obey. Always with younger babies, and often with older ones, the caregiver's approach should be to adjust the situation so that it does not require unreasonable control by the

infant of many of his or her natural reactions. For example, the caregiver may remove the pencil that is being reached for, separate two babies who are pulling each other's hair, or distract a baby who is trying to take a toy away from another baby. With an older baby (over six to eight months), while the caregiver may often simply change the situation to make it easier to deal with, she will also be aware that a baby at that age can begin to learn some controls. The caregiver might, for instance, show an eleven-month-old some ways of interacting with another baby that are likely to be received more positively than pulling hair. Around the age of ten to twelve months, babies can begin to understand that their behavior may produce reactions of approval or disapproval from adults and guide their actions accordingly.

If a day care center provides a program that is designed with babies in mind, most of the limits and prohibitions will have to do with interactions with other people. The physical environment will be such that restrictions on the baby's activities because of safety hazards are at a minimum. A good general guideline for caregivers is that they minimize the number of occasions that call for repeated prohibitions and restrictions. Of course, if this idea were carried to an extreme, it would mean that babies would probably be kept happy at all costs. The goals of a quality day care program, much more complex and far-reaching than merely keeping babies happy or busy, include exploiting appropriate situations to help babies learn self-guidance as they explore. Some examples of ways of minimizing the need for repeated prohibitions and restrictions can perhaps best explain the point.

—A ten-month-old is obsessed with trying to climb up into the rocking chair. His desire to accomplish this far exceeds his ability. The caregiver, who is occupied with feeding another baby, cannot be with him to assist his efforts. She takes the ten-month-old to another part of the room, gives him a toy that interests him, and then removes the rocking chair temporarily from the room until she has time to help him.

—An eight-month-old is playing very busily with a toy that happens to be the favorite of another baby, who cannot sit by and watch this. He crawls over to take it away. The caregiver, understanding that the situation is very frustrating for him, sees this as a good time to involve him in a game with her.

—A seven-month-old has picked up a styrofoam egg carton used as a nesting container for blocks by older babies. He immediately begins chewing on it with great enthusiasm. The caregiver, instead of continuously taking it out of his mouth and encouraging him to play with it in other ways, takes the carton away and gives him a rubber squeeze toy to chew on.

—Several mobile babies insist on crawling through an open door leading into a busy, unsupervised hallway to explore new horizons. The caregiver closes the door rather than repeatedly stopping the babies' efforts to explore.

—The caregiver is preparing lunch in the room for several babies at once, and the process is taking a rather long time. One fussy eleven-month-old pulls herself up to the table and tries to grab the feeding dishes and jars. The caregiver puts her immediately in a feeding table and gives her some finger foods to work with. The caregiver realizes that she should begin earlier to get ready to feed this baby; she cannot expect an alert eleven-month-old to be patient for such a long time after the baby has noticed that she has started getting lunch ready.

—Two babies are together on the floor. One is very irritable and reaches out to pull the other's hair over and over at the slightest frustration. The caregiver perceives that he needs some time alone and puts him in a play pen with some toys.

The common element in all these situations is that the caregiver, sensitive to the baby's limitations, changed the situation according to the baby's needs to make it more tolerable for the baby, rather than expecting him or her to change in behavior.

With older babies, there are some guidelines to help caregivers make a learning experience from a situation where the baby's activities must be redirected. If the caregiver is to help a baby begin to learn to direct his or her own behavior, the adult's interactions with the baby must have a clear meaning for the baby. Therefore, for example, lengthy verbal explanations are largely ineffective in the first year of life. However, an adult's tone of voice can sometimes communicate approval or disapproval effectively before the baby can understand the words. Also, any consequences should follow immediately the undesirable behavior they are intended to influence. For example, separating two older babies immediately after a hair-pulling incident will be more effective than doing it fifteen minutes later. Caregivers have to be sensitive to the limits of the baby's understanding of his or her own behavior.

It is never right for a caregiver to react in anger to a baby. Although a caregiver may become understandably irritated and perhaps even angry with a baby at a particular time, it is important that she not react to the infant in a manner which so clearly reflects anger (as distinguished from irritation or impatience) that the infant may be made anxious or fearful. Physical punishment, such as slapping, pinching, or biting back is most cer-

babies. When younger babies (less than ten to twelve months, approximately) do this, and the "victim" does not mind, it is probably best for the caregiver not to intervene. As babies get older and have more awareness of others, or whenever one of the babies is protesting, the caregiver should intervene in order to redirect energy and attention to help the babies begin to learn ways of interacting that will be pleasant for everyone.

tainly inappropriate and unnecessary for babies and may be harmful.

It should be pointed out that some behaviors which might be undesirable in older children are in babies natural ways of exploring and being curious. When babies first begin to move around, they seem to be interested in each other not as people but as interesting objects to explore. Sometimes the exploring is rough, painful, or at least irritating to the other baby. The caregiver's handling of these episodes will affect the child's feelings about himself or herself, attitudes toward other people, and ideas about exploring. Caregivers should not base their reactions on the assumption that young babies intentionally hurt other babies.

Similarly, it should be recognized that babies have no sense of property rights and are not born with the notion of sharing; therefore, they may take toys from other

Sometimes a caregiver may decide in a certain situation that it is best if she does not intervene right away but gives two babies an opportunity to work things out by themselves. The caregiver would do this only in a situation where she is fairly certain that no one will be hurt. This is often a difficult judgment to make ahead of time.

Even younger babies can be helped to learn to touch and feel other babies in a gentle way. In-

88

stead of removing a baby's hand abruptly from another baby's hair, the caregiver can take the baby's hand and show how to stroke hair, saying something like, "That's right, do it *gently.*" Caregivers do not want to discourage babies from interacting with each other. A baby trying to take a toy away from another baby can be given a duplicate toy that will sometimes be satisfying. The idea is for the caregivers to help the babies work things out satisfactorily. This is more difficult to do before babies understand much language than it will be when they have at least some comprehension of what is being said to them.

When babies are old enough to understand, it is wise to let them know that certain behaviors are discouraged and that the consequences of these behaviors may be unpleasant. These consequences (for example, being temporarily

removed from the play situation) should be carried out consistently, firmly, but without any display of anger. At the same time, the caregiver wants to be sure that she is not encouraging or rewarding undesirable behavior by giving the baby at that time lots of attention or something else enjoyable. The caregiver must be astute enough to sense the occasions when the baby is testing, or teasing her with his behavior, or using it as a way of getting attention, and she must not reward the baby for these behaviors. These situations can be avoided by giving babies adequate attention at other times and responding to their needs quickly and sensitively.

Caregivers must discuss and agree on appropriate reactions to behaviors that are to be discouraged, so that there is some consistency. For instance, if deliberate hair pulling usually is followed by being removed from the play situation for a short period, the baby will eventually learn that the consequences of pulling hair are not pleasant.

One of the habits that parents and caregivers can fall into easily is the misuse and general over-use of *no.* There is often a tendency to use *no* too early and too often, so that it has little or no effect. Often caregivers, busy with a baby and unable to stop what they are doing and intervene directly, will say *no* to a baby from a distance in hopes that the baby will stop. It usually does not work. *No* can become effective when used with an older baby, it seems, only if it is used sparingly and is accompanied by some kind of direct intervention—redirecting the baby, stopping the activity, or removing the child from the scene, for example.

Caregivers should keep in mind that guidance or discipline situations are learning situations, and that coping with a certain amount of frustration and tolerating delays are a part of daily experience. One-year-olds are ready to begin learning this. Caregivers should not and cannot always respond immediately to the baby's requests or always acquiesce to his or her demands. For instance, babies in group care need to learn to tolerate watching other babies eat when they are not eating, without trying to take food. The caregiver might try to help a baby do this by involving the child in an especially interesting activity. One would not expect a hungry baby to watch another eat with any degree of patience, but since this is a realistic life situation, the caregiver would not necessarily try to avoid having it occur. Instead, the adult would try to help the baby cope with the situation, perhaps by helping the baby find something else interesting to do.

The point has been made frequently in this book that effective teaching of babies comes out of understanding normal development and knowing individual babies. Helping babies begin to learn some controls is no different than helping them to gain other kinds of skills. It is important that caregivers view the babies' interactions with the world as a vital part of their development, a part of their emerging interest in acting on the world, in finding out how people and objects work, and how they can best relate to them.

Chapter 6. Helping Babies Adjust—Notes

1. A brief but very good discussion of infant crying in general, and specifically distress related to colic, is contained in the following.

Office of Child Development, U.S. Department of Health, Education, and Welfare. *Infant Care.* Washington, D.C.: U.S. Government Printing Office, 1972. [DHEW Publication No. (OCD) 73-15.] See pp. 17-19.

2. Etzel, B.C., and Gewirtz, J.L. "Experimental Modification of Caretaker-Maintained High-Rate Operant Crying in a 6- and 20-week Old Infant: Extinction of Crying with Reinforcement of Eye Contact and Smiling." *Journal of Experimental Child Psychology* 5 (1967): 303-307.

3. Bell, S.M., and Ainsworth, M.D.S. "Infant Crying and Maternal Responsiveness." *Child Development* 43 (1972): 1171-1190.

4. One of the investigations undertaken as part of our infant nursery research program was an observational study of the frequency of occurrence of infant distress and crying over the period from October 1972, when the infants were four and one half months of age, on the average, to July 1973, when they were thirteen and one half months of age. This study also dealt with an analysis of the apparent reasons for babies' crying and of the procedures used by caregivers in coping with infant crying and distress.

Johnson, J.E. "Crying and the Relief of Distress in an Infant Day Care Nursery." Technical Report, Cornell Research Program in Early Development and Education. Ithaca, N.Y.: Cornell University, January 1974.

5. Brazelton, T.B. *Infants and Mothers.* New York: Delacorte Press, 1969.

6. For a somewhat detailed account of causes of distress in babies, see the following.

Spock, B. *Baby and Child Care.* New York: Pocket Books, 1970 (See Crying, in index).

7. See Chapter 3, note 16.

8. A longitudinal study carried out with our 1972-73 infant nursery sample indicated very infrequent distress reactions (mostly after nine months) when the parent left the infant at the nursery with the familiar caregiver. These infants entered the nursery between two and six months of age, and their reactions to the parent's departure were observed twice weekly over a period of nine months (see report by Willis and Ricciuti, Introduction, note 7). Similarly, in our experimental study of fear and social attachments (Ricciuti, Introduction, note 7) carried out with our 1971-72 group, being left alone by mother with the familiar caregiver produced little or no distress until the twelve-month period, when moderate distress reactions occurred in a few infants, although these were substantially less negative than those observed when the infant was left alone with a stranger. Some distress reactions at being left by the parent at a day care center would be more likely, of course, when an infant is entering such a program for the first time after the age of six months or so, or if an infant is moved from one center to another, or is absent from a center for an extended period of time. In such instances, the situation can be eased considerably if parent and caregiver work together to handle the matter perceptively.

9. Two very good discussions of discipline as it relates to other kinds of learning can be found in the following.

Office of Child Development, U.S. Department of Health, Education, and Welfare. *Infant Care.* Washington, D.C.: U.S. Government Printing Office, 1972 [DHEW Publication No. (OCD) 73-15.] See pp. 33-35.

Keister, M.E. *Discipline: The Secret Heart of Child Care.* Greensboro, N.C.: North Carolina Training Center for Infant-Toddler Care, 1973.

Chapter 7

Routine Caregiving

Much of a caregiver's time in a program for infants is spent in routine or obligatory care routines, namely feeding, diapering, and managing naptime. By understanding that these activities are potentially valuable learning experiences for the baby, the caregiver can use them to accomplish many goals for these infants. Attention is directed in the three sections of this chapter to aspects of care important in the first year of life.[1]*

FEEDING

Feeding is a good example of what might be regarded as a routine or obligatory care activity, but one which serves several important purposes.[2] Besides satisfying the baby's nutritional needs, feeding time offers an opportunity for a young baby to have the caregiver all to himself or herself, to be talked to, to be close. For an older baby, it becomes also a time to find out about new tastes, textures, and colors, to begin to learn names of common objects, to master the difficult job of holding a spoon, maneuvering it into the dish, and balancing it all the way from the dish to that elusive target, the mouth. Learning to hold one's own bottle and eventually to manage a

*Footnotes for this chapter are located on page 107.

spoon and a cup represent early and important achievements in the baby's increasing efforts to master his or her world. The handling of these early attempts at mastery and control by those people caring for the baby lays a base for general attitudes about trying new things, persistence, success and failure.

It is obvious to anyone who has had experience with babies that the nature of the feeding experience changes greatly over the first year of life. The close, peaceful time when a caregiver holds a drowsy baby and gives him or her a bottle soon gives way to a much less serene, more exciting scene when the baby is sitting in an infant seat being given solids. Eventually the baby takes over much of the responsibility for self-feeding, sometimes acting with more enthusiasm than skill. During the second six months of life, the feeding situation becomes much more a social situation with peers, a time to talk with, smile at other babies, and perhaps share food. The feeding situation should be viewed by the caregiver as providing a variety of opportunities for meaningful experiences.

Links with Parents

With babies of any age, feeding is an area of care where the knowledge of what has been happening at home is particularly important. If the caregiver finds out each morning when and how much the baby ate, she will have an idea of approximately when the baby should be hungry again, so that she can interpret the baby's cues more accurately. It is helpful to keep an up-to-date list of foods each baby can eat and any special information about his or her diet, such as special likes and dislikes or food allergies, near the food preparation area. A daily record of when, what, and how much a baby eats should be kept so that the parents can be informed at the end of the day. New foods usually should be introduced at home, at the discretion of the mother, rather than in the nursery. This is one of the particular areas of care where it is the parents' right to make decisions about changes. The amount and kind of table foods a baby eats should be determined by the parents, who may wish to collaborate with the staff before making any decisions.

Parents may have special food requests because of cultural or religious backgrounds. These practices should be respected and made clear to caregivers so they do not violate them. The parents may be asked to provide special foods they want their baby to have. If a parent asks that the baby be given new foods by the caregiver, they should be introduced one at a time. Thus, if an allergic reaction should occur, it will be easier to isolate the cause.

94

Caregivers need to find out from parents when the baby has been given a new food at home, so that they can begin to include it or can watch for an allergic reaction to it. Caregivers should be informed by the parents of any changes in feeding that might be necessary because of minor illnesses.

The information from parents, combined with cues the baby gives and knowledge of the baby's typical schedule, will determine when the caregiver feeds a baby. This approach could be termed a *modified demand schedule*. As in other areas of care, anticipating hunger and feeding the baby before he or she gets upset will make feeding time much more pleasant and relaxed. In younger babies, cues for hunger may include crying or fussiness (especially when the baby has recently had a nap and has been changed), sucking fingers or hands, or just making sucking movements with the mouth. Older babies are less subtle about being hungry—they cry, too, but if possible, they may move over to where another baby is being fed to watch, cry, or try to induce the other baby to share. Of course, the infant may alter his or her feeding schedule for any of a variety of reasons other than how much and how long ago he or she ate. For example, a baby who is ill or teething may suffer a complete or partial loss of appetite. A baby going through a growth spurt may need more frequent feeding or larger amounts than normally required.

It would be easy in a group program, particularly, to misuse food by falling into the habit of using it as a major pacifier to calm a baby and relieve tension. Occasional use of a cracker or bottle to console or comfort a baby is normal and very effective, for eating is a pleasurable experience for most people of any age. However, characteristically using food to quiet an infant in situations where the baby is not hungry can establish an undesirable pattern.

Feeding Time: Caregiver and Baby Together

Especially in a group program, feeding time without preparation can be chaotic, disordered, and no fun for anyone. Planning and awareness of the importance of the setting can be the best preventative measures. If possible, feeding should occur in a relatively quiet place, especially for those babies who are distracted easily by what is going on in the room. The caregiver can be more attentive to the baby or babies she is feeding if she does not have to be constantly surveying the room. As is true in other areas of giving care, the caregiver's enjoyment of the feeding situation can contribute to its being a pleasurable experience for the baby. If the caregiver approaches it with a positive attitude, it is more likely to be fun for the baby, too.

With younger babies, and when a new baby comes to the program, no matter what the child's age, several purposes are served by having the same caregiver feed a baby regularly. In general, this arrangement facilitates their getting to know one another. The caregiver can more quickly learn how fast the baby eats, how much, and the baby's style. For the baby, more time spent in interacting pleasantly with a caregiver will allow the baby to get to know the caregiver as someone to enjoy being with and who can be trusted.

Babies should be held when they are getting a bottle, if possible, even if they are able to hold their own bottles. This is a special time to be close to an adult. Propping bottles in a crib or on a pillow for younger babies is a dangerous and undesirable practice. When younger babies are lying down while eating or drinking, there is the possibility of choking. The practice of putting food (mixed with milk) in a bottle is not recommended. The baby will not get as much food that way because he or she will get tired of sucking. A program in which babies are not usually held when they have their bottles is probably in need either of more caregivers or a discussion of the importance of close one-to-one

contact between babies and adults.

In a group program it is likely that the babies' schedules will be different enough that everyone will not be hungry at the same time. However, it is possible for a caregiver to feed two babies at once and have it be a pleasant experience for all three of them. The kind of feeding required obviously determines how many babies a caregiver can feed at one time. She can feed solids to two babies who are seated in feeding tables or high chairs, and when the babies have started feeding themselves, she can manage more than two.

If a baby rejects a food one day, the caregiver will make a mental note of it and perhaps reintroduce the food in a week or two when the baby is hungry. The caregiver should let the baby determine the pace of the feeding situation and adjust herself to how fast or slowly the baby wants to eat. Especially with young babies, pacing the feeding is a part of individualizing care. Some babies drink very fast and efficiently, while others are slower and may lose interest or become tired before they have had enough to drink. Caregivers should be tuned in to this. Adjusting the size of the hole in the nipple may help to make feeding more relaxed. A baby should not be rushed in his or her eating. Some babies are "nononsense" eaters—that is, they eat at a fast pace, are very businesslike, and seem to encourage the caregiver to be the same. Other babies, who may enjoy the food just as much, are more receptive to talking and socializing during feeding. Caregivers should respect these differences and adjust their behavior to them.

Some very young babies like to assist the caregiver with feeding by putting a hand into the mouth when it is full of solids and grabbing or batting the spoon. A small toy or another spoon will sometimes keep the hands busy. Feeding babies solids is no job for a fastidious caregiver, especially when babies are learning to feed themselves. It is very likely that by the end of the feeding session, the baby, the chair, and probably the caregiver will need to be wiped clean. The caregiver must be careful not to have too high expectations for the baby's competencies. Any feeding situation should be free of unreasonable demands for neatness, attention to the job, and persistence, but caregivers should be especially careful to establish a relaxed atmosphere for babies beginning to learn to feed themselves.

As in other areas, caregivers take cues from the baby's interest in grabbing the spoon or helping to begin letting the baby learn to feed himself or herself. The baby can be given a spoon to hold while being fed. Eventually the baby will accomplish the difficult task of getting it to his or her mouth with food on it. An easier beginning for self-feeding is with finger foods such as

teething biscuits, pieces of cooked carrots or cooked green beans, pieces of mild yellow cheese, or dry cereal. While these do require small motor coordination, they are easier to manage than a spoon. The baby learns to enjoy self-feeding and gains some control over his or her world. These early attempts should be rewarded with enthusiasm and delight by the caregiver. She should encourage the baby's efforts and give help, for instance, in getting the food on the spoon. She should not insist that the baby complete the job alone. Especially when a baby is just beginning to master self-feeding, it is probably wise that the caregiver not rely completely on the baby's efforts to feed himself or herself, for the process may be so difficult that the baby gets tired and quits before eating enough. A better plan is to provide some finger foods at each meal to supplement what is spoon-fed by the caregiver.

The baby's wishes should be respected, in that he or she should not be forced to eat. The caregiver responds to the baby's interest or lack of it. If the baby's loss of appetite persists over several days, parents may wish to check with their physician. The opposite is not true; babies should not be fed every time they ask for food. An older baby may still be smacking his or her lips and protesting as the caregiver removes the dish that ten minutes be-

fore was heaped with food. Babies are subject to suggestion as are older people, and in a group program there will be many times when the sight of another baby eating will cause a baby to ask for food. Caregivers should use discretion with food and should use it when the baby is hungry, not solely to appease, occupy the baby for a few minutes, or to make him or her happy.

When babies have had enough milk, they will generally either refuse to have the bottle in their mouth and start to fuss, or they will start to play with it. They may also allow the excess milk to dribble out the side of their mouth. Once hunger has been satisfied, they may fall asleep. Some babies will suck for a few minutes only, then fall asleep, and awaken in a short time to repeat the cycle. This can be avoided by knowing the baby's schedule and feeding the baby before he or she is sleepy. Talking to babies and playing with their hands and feet or touching the forehead with a damp cloth occasionally will help the babies stay awake. This, of course, does not mean that a baby is ever forced to eat or that feeding time is a frenetic, stimulating time. On the contrary, it should be a relaxed, quiet time. Older babies are not so subtle about telling the adult when they have finished, but will cry, try to get down, turn away, spit the food out, play with it, leave the scene, throw the food on the floor, or refuse to open the mouth. Unmistakable cues! With any group of babies there are likely to be some nutritional problems with allergies or overweight babies, for instance. Caregivers can be very helpful to parents by tactfully suggesting changes in the diet, or that a problem is serious enough to consult the pediatrician.

Quiet play is best after eating, so the baby might sometimes be left in the feeding table with some toys. Older babies, especially those prone to spitting up, should not be put on their stomachs immediately after eating.

Some Practical Considerations

Older babies may want to be fed immediately upon waking up from their nap. At any rate, the sight of someone else eating seems to make them very hungry, so it is best to set up so that several babies can be fed at once. Otherwise, the babies stand around the one who is being fed to beg, borrow, or steal food. By one year, and often as early as six to eight months, most babies are eating three meals a day with perhaps a mid-morning snack of a cracker, piece of cheese, juice, or a piece of fruit. The policy mentioned earlier of not introducing new foods at the nursery without discussing it with the parents should be observed with older babies also.

Babies younger than four to five months are usually fed solids in an infant seat. Individual feeding tables surrounding the baby on three sides, with a flat surface and a raised edge, are good for feeding an older baby solids or letting him or her pick up finger foods himself or herself. An efficient way of handling multiple feeding was worked out at Cornell with the aid of a fairly simple group feeding table, described in Appendix D. If there are self-feeders in the group, the caregiver can supervise the table easily. Food should be kept simple and manageable. As much as possible, all the babies should get the same thing to eat, since the "grass is greener" phenomenon is very true here.

A sheet of plastic under the feeding area makes cleaning easier. Usually the baby will start to drink from a cup at home. When the mother reports this, then a cup will be offered at the nursery. The kind with a weighted bottom and a lid with mouthpiece means fewer spills and easier handling by the child.

Since the kind of milk or formula being used varies quite a bit from baby to baby, it may be best if parents bring each baby's own bottles, carefully labeled, from home each day. If the parents' schedule and work location allow it, arrangements should be made for them to come in, *if they want to*, to

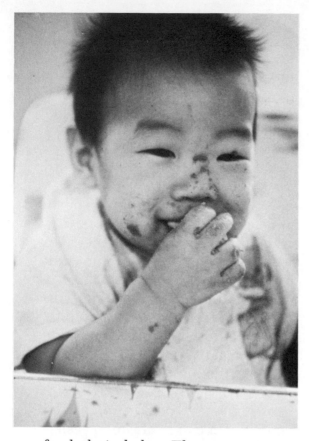

feed their baby. The nursery can stock baby fruits, vegetables, meats, juices, cereals, teething biscuits, and appropriate finger foods. When there are older babies in the program, the variety of foods on hand will need to be greater and will require more planning and preparation by the staff.

Feeding problems in the first year are variable. Many are minor and can be prevented with forethought, planning, and cooperation between staff and parents. Feeding time should be enjoyable, so if a baby is upset or is not interested in eating, the caregiver should be flex-ible enough to postpone feeding until later. She would decide this after some effort with certain babies, however, for not all babies are enthusiastic eaters. New caregivers quickly learn some ways to make feeding easier. Parents of breast-fed babies should give the baby a bottle for at least one feeding regularly at home a few weeks before the baby begins coming to the day care center, so that he or she will be used to getting a bottle. This is helpful even if a mother plans to come in to breast-feed her baby. Some babies show a definite preference for a particular type of nipple or bottle and will drink juice or water much better from the kind they are familiar with. A baby who refuses a bottle should be offered some juice, cereal, or fruit (vegetables or meat depending on age) instead. Mixing a new food or one that the baby is not fond of with one of his or her favorite foods often makes it more palatable.

Babies should not be fed directly from the original jar or container the food came in, but the portion the baby is expected to eat should be put into a dish. This practice will prevent bacteria growth and spoilage; it also means that the food remaining in the original container can be used by another baby. Opened jars of food should not be kept for more than twenty-four hours, even if refrigerated, because of the possibility of contamination and spoilage. All bottles, nipples, spoons, and other eating utensils babies use should be sterilized or washed in an automatic dishwasher. Using disposable bottles for juices assures cleanliness.

Feeding time can be one of the most enjoyable parts of the day for babies and caregivers if it is prepared for ahead of time and carried out in a relaxed way. Some authorities in early child care say that in the first five to six months of life, the feeding experience is perhaps the most important single situation for close contact and interaction between the baby and an adult. This close interaction, when it is pleasant, helps the baby to learn to trust those people who are caring for him or her. This close situation is one where the baby learns early some of the pleasant contingencies, some of the ways he or she can cause something to happen, such as a smile from another person in response to a smile, or words if the baby first coos or babbles. Feeding time should be thought of as a learning time, a fun time, even if just to find out if a thumb can be fitted into a mouth already full of green beans!

DIAPERING

Diapering is an important routine caregiving activity which, properly handled, contributes to the health and comfort of babies. It

can be carried out as a part of the total good experience for the baby, or it can be done as quickly as possible without any special thought. As is true with other routine activities, diapering can be a time for the baby to be talked to and smiled at by the caregiver, as well as to get a dry diaper. As the babies get older, finishing quickly does become important, for the babies do not want to take time out from other activities for a diaper change, and they try to leave before the operation is finished. Sometimes a toy to hold makes the short time more tolerable. The caregiver should be aware of how she is handling the baby at this time, whether her style is abrupt and rough or pleasant and gentle.

As has been mentioned many times, much pleasurable, constructive play takes place in the context of routines. For example, an episode where a caregiver is changing the diaper of a responsive six-month-old baby could easily involve the following experiences for the baby:

Motor activity—kicking vigorously when the caregiver removes confining clothes.

Cognitive activity—the caregiver's face disappears behind the diaper and reappears.

Language activity—caregiver and baby talk, coo, and laugh together.

Social activity—caregiver talks to the baby, laughs with him or her, touches the baby gently, responds to smiles and babbles.

Sensory experience—the feel of being free of clothes, the soft, fresh, dry feeling when a new diaper replaces the cold wet one.

Most importantly, the gentle touch of the caregiver and having a need met without undue delay increases the baby's trust in people. The program is not something that happens only *between* diapering and feeding, but, rather, *during* them as well.

Diapering should be done in a single place in the room—on a diapering table with a rim or in a crib with a high mattress that can be wiped regularly and kept very clean. Otherwise germs and infections can be transmitted easily. A crib is a good place for changing older babies, who are typically very squirmy. No baby should be left unattended for even a second, no matter how young or how certain the caregiver is that the baby cannot roll off the changing table. For this reason, it is best to begin diapering a baby only when there is another caregiver in the room, so that diapering can be completed quickly and without interruption. There should be a supply of diapers, pins, lotion, and wet washcloths easily within reach of the caregiver and out of reach of the baby. The routine at Cornell was that the babies were changed as soon after arrival as necessary. The diaper they arrived in was placed in a plastic bag within a paper bag with the baby's name on it and put in his or her cubby to be taken home. While at the nursery, the babies wore cloth diapers (handled by a laundry service), and shortly before going home they were changed into disposable diapers. Some centers prefer to use only disposable diapers, although one needs to be aware that some babies have allergic reactions to them.

Babies should be checked for wet diapers at least every hour, including before taking a nap and as soon as they wake up from a nap. Babies with a diaper rash should be checked even more frequently. They should be cleaned after each change, and any diaper rash should be treated with an appropriate lotion, salve, powder, or cornstarch. Caregivers must wash their hands before and after *each* diapering. They should remind each other of this, as it is easy to overlook when several babies need diapering at once. As the babies get older, two diapers are used, the inner one being folded to make a four-ply panel down the center.

Some babies mind much less than others wearing a wet or soiled diaper, but that is no reason to allow them to have one any longer than necessary. Caregivers should remember to note changes in bowel movements that might have implications for what the baby eats or how he or she feels. Caregivers should be alert to symptoms of diarrhea, take precautions to prevent its spreading to the other children, and be sure to keep parents informed of symptoms of possible illness.

NAPTIME

In a day care program for babies, sleeping should be handled in somewhat the same way that eating is—that is, by a modified demand approach. Also, like feeding, napping can be handled best when the caregiver knows the baby's schedule and is tuned in to his or her cues. Handling sleeping is different from feeding in some ways, however; a baby who is crying because he or she is hungry rarely becomes more upset when a favorite food is offered, but a fussy, sleepy baby often becomes fussier when put in the crib for a nap. Some babies sleep regularly and go to sleep easily, while others resist sleep from a very early age. Sometimes knowing that the baby *needs* a nap has to determine what the caregiver does, more than whether the baby acts as though he or she *wants* a nap when put down in the crib. Most young babies will take a morning and an afternoon nap. However, this varies from day to day and with individual babies, and many babies drop the morning nap before the end of the first year. An older baby (over six months) typically should not be put down until he or she shows signs of being tired or sleepy.

The normal variability in babies' schedules and needs for sleep and rest makes it inadvisable to have a rigidly set nap period for all babies in a program. There are large differences, even among babies of the same age, in how much sleep they need and when they choose to take naps. These differences should be respected. Individualizing care (Principle 1, Chapter 1) means that caregivers respond to each baby's needs as he or she shows them. It is no doubt possible to eventually get babies to sleep or at least stay in their cribs fairly quietly for a set time each day. However, caring for a child according to a preconceived schedule instead of the cues he or she gives undermines the child's growing sense of self as a person who can indicate needs and have them responded to, who can have an effect on the world. Consideration must be given to what message a child gets when put in his or her crib at a certain time each day no matter how he or she feels. Some people have suggested that one of the reasons many children fight going to bed may be that they have been made to stay in bed at times when they were not tired or sleepy.

If an infant program is housed entirely in one room—that is, if babies nap in the room where they spend their waking time—caregivers may find it useful for both themselves and the babies to try to get them on somewhat the same napping schedule, so that activity in the room will not be distracting to babies resting or sleeping. Also, it is likely that babies in a program will naturally tend to fall into similar sleep patterns. Further, having babies on somewhat similar schedules increases the opportunity for taking the group outside or on excursions, since even one baby sleeping means that a caregiver must be nearby. It is possible, however, for babies to nap outdoors in carriages, playpens, or portable cribs. Some kind of reasonable compromise between completely individualized schedules and a predetermined set naptime for everyone can be worked out in each program. Time away from the babies is very important for caregivers, but breaks should be programmed in at times other than just when babies are napping. Also, some caregivers have noted that the times when only part of the group is awake afford opportunities for play and interaction and for quiet times that are unique.

Naptime is an area of care where consistency in practices from home to nursery and from day to day in the nursery is crucial. The caregiver needs to know each day when and how long the baby slept at home in order to decide wisely when he or she needs a nap. The way a baby is put to sleep at home and in the nursery should be somewhat similar. A goal in a group program should be to help babies go to sleep with little help from the caregiver, as a caregiver for three or four babies cannot always help each one go to sleep individually. A long prenap ritual—

for instance, holding a baby and walking around with him or her for thirty minutes—is just not always possible for every baby in a group program. Also, babies differ widely in how they prefer to be handled at naptime. Some babies, especially very active ones, need a "wind-down" period of quiet play before they can relax and go to sleep. This may mean being placed in a playpen to play quietly, being rocked on a caregiver's lap, or perhaps getting a bottle of juice or reading a book together. The baby may still be awake when put in his or her crib, but the quiet time has been a transition between active play and going to sleep.

Knowing when to begin getting a baby ready to sleep involves a certain amount of second-guessing to choose the optimal period before the baby becomes very fussy but not before he or she is finished playing. Cues that a baby is sleepy may include rubbing eyes, showing disinterest in play, clinging to an adult, sucking a thumb, putting his or her head down, getting clumsy, slowing the pace of activity, becoming frustrated very easily, as well as becoming fussy for no apparent reason.

Just as with eating, the home situation may affect the sleeping routine in the nursery. A parent's absence or guests in the home, for instance, may alter the baby's sleeping schedule. Tension or excitement at home or in the nursery or getting a new tooth may have the effect of making it more difficult for the baby to relax and go to sleep. On the other hand, vigorous physical activity, an oncoming illness, or a period of rapid growth may result in increased napping. A baby who is upset for any reason should not be put down in his or her crib for a nap until having been consoled and comforted. Putting babies in their cribs while they are upset will only make them more upset. Also, most babies cannot go to sleep easily if they are hungry or have a soiled diaper.

Caregivers have to learn not to view naptime as a battle pitting caregiver against baby to see who will emerge the victor. The caregiver should not feel that she has lost if she tries to get a baby to sleep and fails. Caregivers should respond gently and calmly to each baby's needs at naptime, taking time to adjust the naptime routine to each baby.

It is common for some babies to react to being put down for a nap by crying vigorously. Babies differ a great deal in their ability to quiet themselves after this kind of upset. Consistent, predictable handling and allowing the baby to work things out with appropriate support will help the baby develop the ability to put himself or herself to sleep. No set rule can be stated for how long a baby should be allowed to cry in his or her crib before being taken up again. Knowing the baby makes the difference. A caregiver who knows the baby can tell when he or she is past the point of self-quieting. Very often it is more difficult to let the baby cry than to go in and pick him or her up, especially when there are other babies sleeping in the room. A consistent pattern of waiting to put babies down until they are really tired and letting them work things out for themselves sometimes can help them to learn to accept naptime instead of fighting it. Younger babies may need more help than older ones in getting to sleep.

Each baby should have his or her own crib to sleep in each day. The cribs of babies with similar sleeping schedules should be arranged together, and if a large number of babies are napping simultaneously, a caregiver should be assigned to the sleeping room to meet their needs. Otherwise a caregiver should come in periodically to check on the sleeping babies.

Sometimes a baby who will not sleep will rest quietly for a while with a few toys for quiet entertainment in his or her crib. Some babies like to have something to hold onto—a blanket, for instance—when they are going to sleep. Others like the soft sound of a music box or want their pacifiers to put themselves to sleep. Very young babies will nap from thirty

minutes to one and a half hours in the morning, and may nap again soon after eating. As they get older (around six months), the morning nap becomes shorter and may eventually drop out all together. Most babies continue their afternoon nap long after the morning one has dropped out.

Babies should be removed from their cribs as soon as possible after waking up from a nap. Leaving them there will only make naptime unpleasant and lead them to resist it. If they must stay in the same room with babies still napping,

they can be encouraged to play quietly. Naptime should be followed closely by a diaper change. Some babies wake up slowly and need a gradual reintroduction to the brightness and activity of the playroom. If they are brought in immediately after a nap and put down, they will become very upset. A better plan is for the caregiver in a gentle way to pick the baby up, talk softly to him or her, walk around in the sleeping room for a short time, and then go back to the playroom.

Basing naptime routines on the needs and styles of each baby, expecting variations between babies and from day to day, will mean that napping will become a natural, even pleasant activity and not an arena of confrontation.

Chapter 7. Routine Caregiving—Notes

1. There are a number of good sources of information on handling routine aspects of care in the first year and a half of life.

Cohlan, S.Q. *Baby Care: a Program for Self-Instruction.* New York: Instructional Materials Laboratories, 1970.

Fowler, W., and Biderman, E. *Developmental Methods for Physical Care Routines with Infants.* Toronto, Ontario: Ontario Institute for Studies in Education, 1972.

Office of Child Development, U.S. Department of Health, Education, and Welfare. *Infant Care.* Washington, D.C.: U.S. Government Printing Office, 1972 [DHEW Publication No. (OCD) 73-15].

Spock, B. *Baby and Child Care.* New York: Pocket Books, 1970.

2. We have mentioned earlier that this book does not cover in detail the topic of infant nutrition and feeding problems common in the first year and a half of life. Some programs may involve a greater emphasis on nutrition and it will be necessary for caregivers to be very knowledgable in this area. In any program the feeding situation is important, however, and the following references cover both nutrition and the management of feeding.

Appalachian Regional Commission. *Programs for Infants and Young Children. Part II: Nutrition.* Washington, D.C.: Appalachian Regional Commission, 1970.

Bogart, L.J.; Briggs, G.M.; and Calloway, D.H. *Nutrition and Physical Fitness.* Philadelphia: W.B. Saunders, 1973.

This widely used textbook has a good chapter on nutrition in young children (Chapter 20, pp. 457-480). The chapter also has a good set of references.

Department of Health, Education, and Welfare; Maternal and Child Health Service. *Nutrition and Feeding of Infants and Children Under Three in Group Day Care.* Washington, D.C.: U.S. Government Printing Office, 1971 [DHEW Publication No. (HM) 72-5606].

Huntington, D.S.; Provence, S.; and Parker, R.K. *Day Care 2: Serving Infants.* Washington, D.C.: U.S. Government Printing Office, 1971 [DHEW Publication No. (OCD) 72-8. See pp. 42, 43].

Chapter 8

Staff Composition, Training, and Morale

This chapter deals with the most important component in determining the quality of the caregiving practices discussed in the preceding chapters—the competence and motivation of the people who work in the program. The ultimate goal of training caregivers is to help them to be more effective in caring for babies. Three major interrelated concerns of anyone working with a caregiving staff should be (1) to generate and maintain enthusiasm for giving each baby the best possible experience, (2) to provide information in a way that will allow caregivers to understand and appreciate babies more, and (3) to maintain a setting that readily allows caregivers to implement principles of good caregiving in their daily work. Therefore, the content and method of training may include a variety of ways of conveying new skills, providing new insights into the babies' behavior and development, making working conditions more pleasant, and increasing caregivers' excitement about caring for babies. Training as discussed here includes the maintenance of a positive atmosphere and attitude toward daily program operation as well as training in the more traditional sense.

Very generally, the purpose of training is to help caregivers apply in a natural way the principles outlined in this book. The training of all staff members must be a continuing process, not an intensive series of workshops that happens when staff are hired or once a year. Even the best workshop series can have only a temporary effect. Important new information must be presented in a variety of ways again and again if it is to have a lasting effect on caregiving practices. No matter what the topic or the form it takes, training should be tied very closely to what is going on currently in the program. If topics for the further education of caregivers come directly from problems and questions that arise from working with the babies, then new information and suggestions can be applied immediately and are not pushed aside in the face of more urgent concerns. For example, a discussion of infants' social attachment to adults and possible negative reactions to strangers is not very relevant for a staff working with a group of very young babies (two to five months old). That topic would be much more meaningful at a time when some babies actually begin to react negatively to unfamiliar people.

The first section of this chapter deals with the general categories of personnel needed to staff a day care program and descriptions of their roles. An overview of the form and content of training for both new and experienced caregivers will follow. A very important determinant of caregiver—and, more generally, program—effectiveness is staff morale. The degree to which staff members enjoy working with each other, their satisfaction with working conditions, and their level of participation in program planning and execution contribute significantly to the overall quality of the program. Therefore, the final section of this chapter will deal with the issue of staff morale.

DESCRIPTION OF STAFF POSITIONS

The kinds of staff employed for a day care program for babies depend on many factors—size of the total program, finances, and goals.[1]* A program designed to do more than provide quality day care—for instance, one whose scope also includes working with parents in the home, providing comprehensive health services, or helping families reach other social agencies—would require additional staff positions. The following descriptions of staff positions are not prescriptive, but, rather, are intended to indicate general categories of skills and resources needed to operate a quality program. The job responsibilities described below could be grouped differently—that is, a director of a day care center that includes an infant program might function on a

---

*Footnotes for this chapter are located on pages 130-131.

110

part-time basis as a trainer of caregivers or in other capacities suggested as the program director's role. Consultants and resource people from outside the program can also be used in many capacities as trainers or technical consultants.

The following kinds of positions are necessary to staff a day care program for infants:

1. **Program Director.** The director has major responsibility for determining, with the cooperation of parents and sponsoring agencies, the philosophy, objectives, and the guidelines of the program, as well as their implementation. The largest areas of involvement of the program director are in staff recruitment and training and in maintaining the quality of the program. She should have a strong background in early childhood education and child development (for example, the equivalent of a master's program) and experience in working in programs for very young children and infants. Perhaps it is very unrealistic to suggest that each center should have such a person in charge, and it may not be necessary in all instances. However, it is crucial that, if not part of a center staff, such a person have a close continuing relationship with each individual center within a larger program—city-wide, for instance. The program director must be thoroughly familiar with the programs he or she works with and an active participant in them. The program director should function so that he or she is *not* thought of as a consultant, someone who comes in periodically to check up on the program and then leaves. Familiarity means knowing the program not only by watching it and talking about it, but also by participating in it. Substituting occasionally for an absent caregiver is a good way to get a feeling for what is happening.

The program director is responsible for major policy decisions such as the number of children that can be accommodated, budgeting, and major purchases.[2] He or she is in charge of hiring and firing staff and assessing their competencies and needs. The program director serves very naturally as a "troubleshooter," a person to whom any problem can be brought and considered, if it cannot be worked out at a different level. He or she should work closely with the principal caregiver on questions of management of the daily program.

One of the most important concerns for the program director is not to assume responsibilities that others could handle more appropriately. Staff members at all levels should be given as much responsibility as they are capable of assuming. One of the most vital contributors to maintaining a good relationship with staff is developing confidence in them and fostering their confidence in themselves as well as in the program director. Caregivers should not be made to feel that they are puppets who only implement what they are told to do. They, as well as other staff members, should be encouraged to make decisions themselves about matters that are in their domain. This makes their job more interesting and exciting, and the operation of the program more efficient. Decisions can be made quickly and problems solved.

For the next five years at least, day care programs for infants and toddlers will probably continue to be relatively uncommon, and therefore will attract many visitors. The program director will have some responsibilities for talking with visitors and also ensuring that other staff members are familiar enough with all aspects of the program that they can show visitors around and answer their questions.

2. **Principal Caregiver.** One of the caregivers should be designated as the principal caregiver. Her job includes functioning as a caregiver, as well as additional responsibilities. The principal caregiver, more than any other staff member, is primarily responsible for the smooth day-to-day functioning of the center. It is she who can work with the other caregivers to solve problems that come up with parents—seeing that they pick their children up on time, for instance.

To a greater degree than the program or center director, she is totally immersed in the daily program and can get from that a valuable perspective on strengths and needs. In some programs, an individual might serve as the supervising caregiver and assume many of the responsibilities described above for the program director.

The principal caregiver is someone with considerable experience in caring for babies and children. She should exemplify the kinds of caregiving practices the program is aiming for and be able to articulate them, since she will be a teacher of new caregivers. The principal caregiver is an indispensible link between all the caregivers and other staff members, and she should work with the program director, communicating problems or needs expressed by the caregivers or based on observation. The principal caregiver should participate very actively in staff training, as one who knows better than anyone else what the needs in this area are.

Many managerial responsibilities can be coordinated through the principal caregiver. Small purchases and working out arrangements with parents are jobs that require time but are necessary. The principal caregiver can take over the job of approving absences of caregivers and finding substitutes for absent caregivers. She should be the one to interview parents applying for the program, explain it thoroughly to them, answer their questions, and be ultimately responsible for deciding to accept them into the program or not.

3. **Caregiver.** Providing quality care for infants is the main topic of all the chapters of this book, so a brief sketch of the major aspects of caregiving should suffice here. First, of course, it is the caregiver's responsibility to care for the babies while they are at the center. In order to do this effectively, she must talk with the parents each day, both to give them information and to get information about the babies from them. If special problems arise concerning the baby or communication with the parents, she can turn to the principal caregiver and the program director for help. Caregivers are responsible for setting up for the day—getting food trays ready, folding diapers, making beds, selecting toys, setting up charts for parents to write down information about the baby. Makeup of staff will vary from center to center, but it is probably necessary for caregivers to assume some responsibility for cleaning up at the end of the day—stripping beds, straightening the playroom, washing toys and eating utensils, sterilizing bottles.

Since the caregivers will be most closely acquainted with needs, they should be in charge of purchasing food and other maintenance supplies. As a part of pro-

gram planning, caregivers should be the ones who determine needs for toys and other small equipment to make life more interesting for themselves and babies. They can also handle purchasing or making these toys. Caregivers will no doubt have other responsibilities in the areas of record keeping, program planning, or training. Caregivers, as people who know the babies' needs best, should feel that they are a vital source of input to the total program.

The beginning level of training and skills in potential caregivers is not nearly so important as is "teachableness," an openness and willingness to learn. The skills can be learned on the job by a motivated, sensitive person. The caregivers in the Cornell program developed a list of characteristics they thought a caregiver should have.

Possession of some of these qualities is more important in a caregiver than is a lot of previous experience with babies and children. It should be pointed out that some of them are motivational characteristics (qualities to be worked for) rather than competencies already attained.

Three kinds of qualities can be listed—program-related, baby-related, and parent-related:

QUALITIES NECESSARY FOR WORKING IN A DAY CARE PROGRAM

1. Good physical and mental health.

2. Sense of humor (sometimes laughing is the only way to cope).

3. Self-confidence coupled with flexibility, willingness to change, ability to accept and offer criticism.

4. Openness to new ideas, motivation to learn.

5. Maturity that combines accepting the fact that many days are the same, and an ability to get excited about little things, to appreciate small accomplishments.

6. Efficiency and adaptability, the ability to function under pressure, to be calm in less than calm conditions.

QUALITIES NECESSARY FOR WORKING EFFECTIVELY WITH BABIES

1. Patience—babies are sometimes noncooperative.

2. General knowledge about babies and early development.

3. Perserverance coupled with patience.

4. Fondness for babies.

5. Interest in getting to know each individual baby.

6. Perceptiveness, the ability to take the role of the other, to see the world through the baby's eyes—this means compassion at teething times, for instance.

7. Warmth that is expressed in ways that are noticed by babies.

8. Creativity in play, being able to come up with interesting ways to show the world to babies.

QUALITIES NECESSARY FOR WORKING WITH ADULTS

1. Respect for and tolerance of differences of opinion.

2. Tact.

3. Acceptance of others' strengths and weaknesses.

4. Investment in promoting parental confidence.

5. Empathy, an ability to see the parents' or another caregiver's point of view.

Experience of some kind with babies is crucial for a potential caregiver to have, for that is the only way she can know if she *likes* babies (not all people do!). Past education or training are *not* as crucial, though, as the qualities listed above. People with warmth, who find babies exciting and are open to learning, are the ones who tend to become excellent caregivers.

In thinking about the fit of a person in a job as caregiver, it is important to remember that an eight-week-old baby is very different from a six-month-old, who bears little resemblance in many ways to a twelve-month-old. They demand different kinds of care and give very different kinds of responses in return. Therefore, any one person may not be equally effective with babies of different ages.

4. **Substitute Caregiver.** Several people available on short notice should be on call in case of a caregiver's illness or absence. They should have the qualifications demanded of regular caregivers and should participate in at least some of the training. A substitute care-

115

giver will be little more than an extra pair of hands if she is not familiar with the babies and they with her. Therefore, it would be wise for her to spend some time regularly with the children and the regular caregivers (perhaps an hour or two a week). If staff meetings are scheduled at the center, this would be a time for some substitute caregivers to help out and at the same time to become familiar with and to the babies.

5. **Health Personnel.** The staff of a day care program must have easy access to health personnel, not only in case of emergencies, but to ensure that health standards and policies regarding sick babies are maintained. One alternative to having a nurse assigned to the program on at least a part-time basis is to designate one caregiver as the health resource person and ensure that she receives training for that role. The best arrangement is for one of the caregivers to have had nursing experience, for she already has a close day-to-day relationship with the babies. The nurse will be in charge of health records. If she is not at the center on a full-time basis, she will have to train the caregivers to look for symptoms of illness in the children and to respond appropriately to them. The health resource person will establish health guidelines for the center for both staff and children, as well as first aid and emergency procedures. In the capacity as trainer and information-giver to staff and parents, the nurse provides reading material and topics for discussion.

If a nurse is available on a regular basis, it is necessary only to have a physician on call. However, the physician should be acquainted with the children in the center by making periodic visits. His or her advice would be needed less frequently than the nurse's, of course, but would be necessary at times. The physician too, would play an important role in educating staff about issues related to health.

6. **Custodial Help.** A person to do large maintenance jobs — cleaning floors and rugs, washing windows—might be necessary on only a part-time basis. There are times when minor repairs on equipment or an idea for a new toy demand skills in carpentry, electrical wiring, engineering.

7. **Clerical Help.** This person will handle finances, order supplies, do bookkeeping, and other routine clerical work.

TRAINING: HOW AND WHAT?

It has already been said that training must be ongoing, that caregiving should be done with an attitude of creativity, an openness to new and more effective ways of caring for babies. The following discussion applies to both new and more experienced caregivers working in a program.

The kind of training program being proposed here is essentially an informal one that includes planned workshops, readings, and lectures to convey factual information, but which puts major emphasis on an attitude of questioning, learning, and growing on the part of the caregivers. Caregivers must have a large body of factual information and a number of specific caregiving skills if they are to function effectively. Equally important, however, are staff morale and the degree of excitement and enthusiasm caregivers have about their responsibilities.[3]

If the atmosphere is one where caregivers are not defensive about their work and feel comfortable talking about what they are doing and problems they are encountering, many learning experiences will happen informally. There should be, in addition, a specified time at least once a week for caregivers to talk about caregiving, especially about specific babies. Talking about a baby's style, likes and dislikes, and skills is perhaps the best way to help caregivers get to know their babies. Each person will contribute from a somewhat different perspective, and everyone becomes more sensitive to the baby.

There should be built into programs opportunities for caregivers to brag about their work, to talk about activities that succeeded. Occasions of this kind free them to be more critical in a constructive way about their work and those plans and activities that may not have been so successful.

Methods of Training

Most significant learning experiences for caregivers take place out of the setting of scheduled meetings or lectures. Talking over problems and situations as they are taking place makes more impact than a discussion later. The person responsible for training should spend a lot of time observing and working with both babies and caregivers. Simply demonstrating a new way of interacting with or responding to a baby may or may not be effective. Very often the demonstration will be lost in the busy atmosphere of the nursery. What will be retained may not be the possibility of a new way of relating to a baby, but rather only that someone came in and helped. Subtlety and tact are important characteristics for someone training caregivers, but an approach based on the thought that "If I handle the situation in a better way, maybe she will pick up the hint without my saying anything" may not be successful. Suggestions and ideas must be

117

made explicit. Only then can a demonstration be assured of effectiveness. All of this is not to say that caregivers do not learn by watching others. On the contrary, this is probably the most effective way of learning *when it happens.* The problem is that learning in this way may be "hit and miss."

There are some guidelines that can help to ensure that a new caregiver will learn by watching an experienced caregiver work. First of all, the situation must be one where the person being trained is free to observe. A new caregiver who has responsibility for several babies is not likely to have time to watch another caregiver. Secondly, the "model" caregiver must see herself as functioning in a teaching role, as needing to talk about what she is doing. Third, a certain amount of background and knowledge of what to look for is necessary. For instance, a new caregiver must be aware of persistence as a characteristic to be encouraged in babies. Only then can the caregiver learn from watching another caregiver playing with a baby who is trying to move to a toy that is just out of reach. Many of the most sensitive and important caregiving acts are very subtle in their sensitivity— therefore, a trained person should be present with a new caregiver while she is observing to point out what is happening. Discussion of observations is vital if they are to be a meaningful component of a training program.

One of the most effective methods of staff training is the informed discussion. Many problems and topics that arise in caring for babies do not have simple correct answers, and caregivers may disagree on answers and solutions. This situation can be used advantageously, however, since everyone's opinion should be respected. In such a discussion, the staff knows ahead of time what the topic will be, and each person is asked to think about it and perhaps write some notes. The clear expectation is that everyone will have some thoughts to contribute. A staff will undoubtedly be composed of people from different backgrounds, varying educational levels, and a diversity of experiences with babies and children. It is the job of the person in charge of staff training to establish an atmosphere where it is clear that information based on personal experience is as valid and acceptable as knowledge from formal education, academic experience, or child development literature. For many issues in child care, there are no clearly correct answers, but only a variety of opinions.

A discussion should have a focus and direction. The person in charge should steer the discussion, but be flexible enough to change the plan. It is very easy for a discussion about babies to stray from the central issue. Issues, questions, a choice between alternatives lend themselves to a discussion session better than do attempts to convey information, to establish facts. It is best to choose a topic that everyone knows something about or has an opinion on. While there is room for differences in caregiving practices, it is important that a staff agrees on many basic policies that affect their caregiving. Consistency from day to day and from person to person means that the baby is not exposed to extreme variations in response from the caregivers. There will have to be many individual compromises by caregivers for the sake of consistency. For instance, caregivers may disagree on how they should react to certain kinds of distress, but it might be very important for the baby's learning that they respond in similar ways. Agreeing on many basic issues still leaves much room for individuality on the part of caregivers.

Staff meetings provide opportunities for presenting new factual information or reviews of familiar topics by outside speakers or a staff member who is an expert in a particular area. Setting aside a regular time for training and for discussing problems helps to create and maintain a learning, growing outlook on the job of caregiving. Caregivers will be encouraged to work with an eye on improving, questioning, doing things a better way.

Providing appropriate reading material and a time and place to read it is another way to encourage caregivers to think about what they are doing. Articles from newspapers and popular magazines are often controversial and will provoke discussion. Caregivers can take advantage of short breaks to do some reading. Relying on breaks is not enough, however. They are often sporadic, too brief, and too interrupted to allow concentration. Some time should be set aside specifically for reading. What is being read should be talked about and used.

Visits to other facilities are usually enjoyable and enlightening. There is a great value in seeing programs that are similar to or very different from one's own. The process of comparing and contrasting philosophies and practices gives a stronger sense of what one's own program is like. Essentially, it defines it and increases the staff member's sense of identity with the program. Caregivers enjoy comparing notes on daily operation and routines and inevitably pick up new ideas for caregiving.

Providing caregivers opportunities to teach and do training themselves, either with other members of their staff or outside people (parents, for example), is one of the most effective ways of giving them an awareness of their expertise and competence, as well as encouraging them to grow in their knowledge.

The Content of Training

As for what should be the content of training, the answer is almost anything of interest. Many topics for training are the ones covered in this book—the principles and practices of good care for babies. In several areas—namely, nutrition and health—the contents of this book must be supplemented with more complete information from other sources. In addition, training must encompass a number of related issues—what babies are like, how one best cares for babies, what researchers have found out about early development, how a group of people from diverse social, racial, ethnic, educational, and economic backgrounds can get along well and learn from each other, how cultural practices or those requested by parents might influence a baby's behavior and development.

Most topics fall into three main categories: (1) infant development, (2) understanding individual babies, and (3) daily routines and play activities. The importance of caregivers knowing about normative development, the usual course of events, has been stressed many times in this book. Not only does this information help them to interact more effectively with babies, but it gives them a keener insight

and thus a greater appreciation of the babies' emerging skills. This, in turn, should generate greater enthusiasm and interest in caregiving. Some exposure to child development literature—the research and theories behind the research—adds interest, even though it may not directly affect caregiving practices. For instance, an overview of different ideas about why babies become attached to their mothers may not have any direct bearing on how caregivers take care of the babies, but it helps them become more perceptive, and gives greater insight into the babies' behavior.

If caregivers are to individualize care, it is absolutely necessary to set aside time to talk about individual babies. These discussions may be tied closely to a more general look at early development as caregivers discuss what babies are doing now and getting ready to do. The focus of the discussion should always be such that caregivers are not thinking in terms of how individual babies deviate from or fail to measure up to developmental norms; but rather that caregivers are sharpening their sensitivity to each baby's style and pace of development with the aim of individualizing care more effectively and enhancing the baby's development.[4]

The third area of concern in training is that of the daily opera-

120

tion of the program, an "umbrella" covering a wide range of topics such as nutritional concerns in infancy, room arrangements, common illnesses in the first year of life, responding appropriately to babies' distress, ideas for new play activities or materials. A list of topics that lend themselves well to discussion includes an analysis of toys and their value for babies, issues that come up in relating to parents, what to do about a baby who inadvertently hurts other babies by actively exploring them, the use and misuse of *no* with babies, appropriate goals to have in caring for babies.

Learning by doing is as effective with adults as it is with babies. Having caregivers plan and make some of the toys and equipment serves several purposes: (1) it adds an additional dimension of involvement for caregivers; (2) often the results are more durable, more interesting, and safer toys; (3) it may save money; (4) as a tool for staff training, it allows thinking about the babies' interests and skills and planning toys to match them, rather than working from the opposite direction.

In the beginning of a program or whenever new caregivers are being trained, the topics of training will, of course, be very basic ones. The wisest course is to make explicit even seemingly trivial or very obvious points about caregiving.

What caregivers already know may not be dealt with in detail, but mentioning the whole range of good practices points them out as important and validates them for even the experienced caregiver as a good thing to do. Initial training sessions should be concerned with topics such as feeding; crying and relief of distress; the importance of relaxed, consistent handling; babies' needs for affection; ways of playing with young babies; and developmental landmarks in the first year.

Use of This Book in Training

It was stated in the introduction to these guidelines that the philosophy behind the authors' approach to training caregivers for babies is that caregivers should become aware of some basic principles of good care which are linked with many concrete examples from their daily experience. The twelve principles that constitute the framework of this book are the rationale and the philosophy that are implicit in all the training done with both new and experienced caregivers. The goal of a training program would be to have caregivers adopt these principles and, more importantly, to develop the skills and perceptiveness that will allow them to translate the principles into the way they live each day with babies.

The general approach to train-

ing recommended here involves as a first step being certain that caregivers have an understanding of what babies are like in the first year of life, how development proceeds. Once this common knowledge base is established, the principles of this book should be presented as a context into which to fit the specific caregiving skills and techniques that will constitute the major part of training. Caregivers should have copies of the principles so that they can become familiar with them.

Competent caregiving includes general perceptiveness

about babies, plus a vast number of specific skills in the areas outlined in this book. The major part of training will be devoted to topics like feeding, diapering, handling distress, working with parents. The information contained in these guidelines is intended as a starting point, a basis for consideration of many other sources of information on specific topics, some of which are listed in the Chapter Notes. As stated earlier, this book is intended for persons involved in setting up and operating infant programs, and where appropriate, can be studied directly by caregivers. With some groups, trainers might find it useful for each caregiver to have a copy of the book. The most crucial component of this kind of training is that the concrete information about very basic skills, the carrying out of routines, be linked back to the principles. Basically the process is one of making the principles meaningful *inductively*. For instance, telling a person who is preparing to work with babies for the first time that *every experience should be a learning experience* may be meaningless. However, during a good training program the adult will learn among other things that caregivers should talk to babies when diapering them; lunch time offers an excellent opportunity to practice fine motor skills (picking up peas is a real challenge for an eight-month-old); sometimes when a baby is upset the caregiver will not react immediately but will give the baby a chance to work things out himself or herself; the room should be arranged to help babies discover new places and objects to explore. These concrete facts and skills together define what is meant by *every experience is a learning experience.*

The links between the concrete facts of how to carry out a program and the rationale behind the facts must be emphasized over and over. This linkage serves two purposes: Caregivers come to appreciate the importance of what they are doing, and, secondly, the principles will generate new ways of caring effectively and sensitively for babies. A goal of training should be that caregivers will eventually be able to make the links themselves.

Tools for Training

In keeping with the idea of training as an ongoing process, there are some tools and procedures that can be used by and with caregivers to increase sensitivity to individual differences in babies. Three ways of incorporating occasions for caregivers to focus on individual babies are suggested: rating scales, a check list of developmental landmarks, and the use of developmental assessments. It should be noted that to recommend that these be used is highly unrealistic in a minimally staffed program, where caregivers work with babies all day and are not given time out of the nursery to do other kinds of work related to caregiving.

The first tool is a set of rating scales (Appendix E) covering dimensions of babies' behavior important in the first year of life. The seven rating scales used by the caregivers in the Cornell program focus on the following characteristics.

1. Affectivity—the degree of pleasure or displeasure shown by the baby over the day.

2. Persistence—how hard the baby works when confronted with a problem or some obstacle to overcome.

3. Level of Attention—the intensity of involvement in activities.

4. Sensitivity—how easily the baby is upset by changes in the environment.

5. Activity—how busy the baby is; how much he or she does.

6. Quieting and Consolability —how easily the baby is soothed after becoming upset.

7. Initiation of Exploration—the extent to which the baby is assertive in interacting with the world of objects; the degree to which the baby is a self-starter.

These are some of the major dimensions on which babies differ in the first year of life and which determine how they will be cared for. Most of them have been alluded to in other contexts as they influence program planning and individualization of care. Apart from the scales' value in giving information about changes over time or as a result of changes in the caregiving environment or differences between babies, the scales provide for a caregiver a way of looking at babies, a framework to use to get to know them. Having to rate a baby on each of these scales two or three times a week channels the caregiver's thoughts along these dimensions, and she soon comes to view babies in terms of these characteristics. Left to choose their own dimensions, caregivers would be more likely to focus on obvious, more global characteristics. Each person would undoubtedly choose some unique dimensions, and a common basis for talking about individual babies would be missing.

The caregivers in the Cornell program found the scales useful as a way to get to know individual babies, but after a period of a couple of months they observed that the characteristics contained in the rating scales had become such a natural part of the way they viewed the babies that the actual process of doing the ratings was no longer helpful. They did not think that doing the ratings added any new information, since discussion of the babies in the nursery and at staff meetings always revolved around the dimensions of behavior contained in the rating scales. Their recommendation, therefore, was that rating scales should be used on a new baby for eight to ten weeks, and by a new caregiver for a similar period of time, as a way of channeling thinking about babies.

A list of developmental landmarks can be used effectively in conjunction with developmental assessments to help caregivers maintain sensitivity to each baby's development. The check list used at Cornell (Appendix F) contains some of the major milestones in the first year and a half of life. Caregivers are asked to familiarize themselves with the items and to mark down the approximate date of first occurrence and repeated occurrences. Competent caregivers are aware of the approximate age these behaviors occur in most babies, and they know that extreme deviations should be taken seriously, but they do not view the landmarks as skills to get the baby to do early or even on time, unless the baby wants to.

124

These tools must be used very cautiously and in the context of individual differences. Well-intentioned enthusiasm on the part of a caregiver may lead her to devote an inordinate amount of time to a particular aspect of development and neglect others. Very few babies adhere exactly to developmental norms. Also, caregivers should be sensitized to appreciate developmental progress in different modalities, not just the obvious large motor skills. Visual, manipulative, and social skills are equally important, though less obvious.

Caregivers should understand that acceleration in one area of development may not indicate anything unusual in other areas. *It will also be necessary to emphasize the point that acceleration per se— teaching a six-month-old baby a skill that most babies have at eight months, for instance—can be accomplished but is not a particularly desirable goal and may even be meaningless.* At present, the evidence researchers and educators provide does indicate that many lags in development can be compensated for, but it has not been shown that normal development can be speeded up in any lasting or significant way. This is not to say that all babies have equal potential. However, what is desirable for a caregiver to know is a baby's strengths and weaknesses, where he or she is developmentally and where the baby is going, what adults can do to facilitate development. To allow caregivers to set developmental norms as absolute standards that every baby should measure up to or as exercises to drill each baby with, or to let them become competitive about which baby develops a certain competency first would do more harm than good. However, providing a relaxed situation to engage the baby in activities and to help caregivers take note of how a baby is progressing, what skills are becoming part of his or her repertoire, and what a baby can do now that could not be done several weeks ago, can only serve to increase their enjoyment of their role.

Developmental assessments may be useful in some centers as another way of helping caregivers focus their attention on changes in individual babies over time. They must be used cautiously. The developmental assessment used may be any of several standardized tests.[5] It must be administered by a trained tester. Its appropriate function in a day care program, however, is not to compare babies or to see if the program has any effects on the babies' performance on the test. It is, rather, another way to help a caregiver get to know a baby, to focus on the child's progress and on particular strengths and weaknesses.

In the Cornell program, test

scores were never discussed, but the tester used the session to call attention to the babies' skills, to ask the caregiver questions that would sharpen her sensitivity to the baby. The assessments were not used diagnostically except as they pointed out indirectly to the caregiver new ways to play with the baby or a new awareness of a baby's skills. Responsibility for the use or misuse of developmental tests lies primarily with the tester, who interprets to the caregiver what the baby is doing. The optimal situation is one where the tester and baby are familiar with one another. Not only does this allow the testing to proceed much more smoothly, but knowing the baby in a natural setting gives the tester a broader base of knowledge for assessing performance in a testing situation. Again, the misuse of these tests could be very harmful to a program, and great caution should be exercised in their use.

Training New Caregivers

The discussion thus far has dealt primarily with continuous, ongoing training that is necessary to establish and maintain a quality day care program for babies. Some attention must be paid to the training of a new caregiver—someone who has had little or no previous experience with babies. How should a new person be brought into a program and helped to become a competent, sensitive caregiver? Initial training should have four components occurring simultaneously: (1) caregiving supervised and directed by experienced caregivers who see themselves in a teaching role and who will talk about the babies and what they are doing; (2) time to observe the program, specifically the caregivers' actions; (3) appropriate reading material on early development and day care programs; (4) discussions with the program director and the caregivers about the first three components of training as well as program policies and individual babies. Admittedly, a new caregiver will be overwhelmed with all the information she needs to know and the skills she needs to master immediately in order to function at all. She should be forewarned that she will feel this way, and that she will not be expected to function without help and without asking a lot of questions for many, many weeks.

It is strongly recommended that new caregivers be hired for a trial period of apprenticeship in which they can decide if they like the job and their potential can be observed and evaluated. It is impossible to determine that a caregiver will work well with babies without seeing her work with babies. Caregivers may work more effectively with one age group than

126

another, and this should be taken into account in hiring and evaluating performance. It is crucial that there be established from the beginning an honest, open relationship between all staff so that a good learning situation can be set up. Expectations for a new caregiver must be reasonable, and experienced caregivers must be very patient as they teach and work with someone with less experience. The babies will not be patient! A new caregiver needs a lot of support as well as instrumental help from the adults she works with, for the babies will give her honest feedback about her present skills. The program director (or principal caregiver), while she will serve in a sense as a monitor, one who spots problems and suggests solutions, must be seen as an ally of caregivers old and new, who points out instances of good caregiving as well as areas where things could be done better.

There is a potentially undesirable consequence in formal training, in making explicit the components of good caregiving. That danger is that caregivers will become overly self-conscious and lose their spontaneity. Training should allow for individual differences in caregiving styles. Caregivers should act naturally, and there should be not merely a tolerance of individual differences, but encouragement of them, within the limits

of good care. Whenever the opportunity arises, someone should point out to caregivers that many of the things that they do spontaneously and naturally are those kinds of experiences that are thought to be most important for babies.

MORALE

Throughout this discussion of staff composition and training, and, in fact, throughout the entire book, one of the key concepts which is repeated in many different contexts is *communication*—communication between caregivers and babies, caregivers and parents, caregivers and other caregivers. This third kind of communication is critical if morale is to be high. Staff morale, in turn, plays as large a role as does staff competence in determining the quality of a program. *A well-trained caregiver who is unhappy with working conditions or is not getting along with another staff member or who feels powerless to affect decisions about her job is not likely to do a good job caring for babies.* A caregiver cannot focus on meeting babies' needs when her own are not being met. Enjoyment—happiness—cannot be trained in, but comes as a by-product of good communication and satisfaction with one's job. A person responsible for hiring new staff members cannot know in most cases how well or how poorly a person is going to get along with other staff. A new staff member must *fit together* with the rest of the staff, which is not quite the same thing as *fitting in*. Fitting together is something, like training, that must be worked at continuously. Because it is rather nebulous and impossible to train in, morale often gets a minimal treatment or is not mentioned in training manuals. It is so important, though, that any discussion of components of a quality day care program is incomplete without it.

Morale may be low for one of many reasons pertaining to problems in the program. It is likely, however, that sometimes caregiving settles down to a dull roar— everything is under control, nothing new is happening—and caregivers become bored, even though they may be very busy. The feeling that nothing is happening comes from the sameness in routines of caring for babies day to day. Feelings of discontent are very contagious—one caregiver's mood can spread quickly to other staff members. It is at this time that a perceptive program director will introduce something new, change the routine, involve the caregivers in a project they will find interesting.

When caregivers are unhappy, they cannot interact as effectively with the babies as they do when they are feeling good. There will be

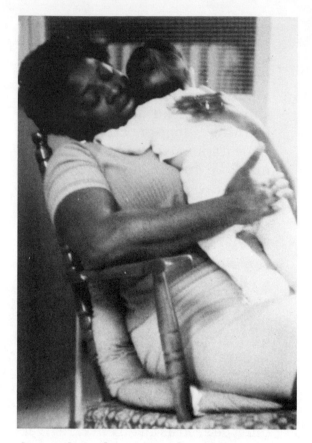

days when, because of pressures at home or other personal problems, a caregiver does not do her best. On the other hand, there will be days when she is being a very competent, enthusiastic caregiver, and the baby is just not responding. Not only is the baby failing to show any appreciation at all, but also he or she is doing all the wrong things— crying when he or she should be cooing contentedly or laughing happily, wetting the diaper five minutes after a change, refusing food, acting sleepy but yelling when put in his or her crib. Babies sometimes have bad days (or even bad weeks), too! Caregivers should be forewarned that these days occur. There is no magic solution for coping with them. Being able to admit that it is a bad day and being able to laugh about it helps. A sense of humor is very necessary for a caregiver! It is difficult to have a sense of humor by oneself. Again, communication, good rapport between people who work together, is important. A bad day shared and laughed about with another person is better than a bad day suffered alone.

A happy atmosphere, good relationships among staff members and with parents, quickly filters down to the babies. *Caregivers need to be more than child-centered; it is equally important that they be oriented to the moods and needs of fellow workers.*

If the atmosphere in the program is one of constantly learning and becoming, doing a better job, not only will people be more excited about their work, but there will be less need for defensive attitudes. If caregivers can be open about problems or questions they have, if there are channels for constructive criticism as well as praise, then there will be no need for seething undercurrents of discontent that can impair effectiveness. Very generally, people working as closely together as caregivers, sometimes in very tense, irritating situations, must get along well with each other. They do not have to agree always, but they must understand their differences and like each other in spite of them. Competent, sensitive caregiving is very much a team effort.

Another major contributor to high morale is the degree to which caregivers are involved in program planning, the extent to which they have an effect on decisions that are made. They should be included in any decision making that affects their work. In the same way, they should be given as much responsibility as they have time for, desire, and are competent to handle. Working with parents, making purchases, planning staff and parent meetings are all areas where caregivers should have some input. Extra responsibilities should be given and accepted with the understanding that the caregiver's primary job is to care for babies. Additional responsibilities should not detract from this in any way.

Staff morale can be affected by very simple changes—the addition of a new piece of equipment, giving someone a couple of hours off or even an extra thirty-minute break, or telling a caregiver that she did a good job. These are important and can make the difference between a mediocre day and a very good day for a group of babies and caregivers.

All dimensions of caregiver functioning and morale are facilitated or impeded by the scheduling of caregivers' working hours. Of course, the situation will be somewhat different in each program, but a few general recommendations can be made. It has been stated previously that, no matter what the size of the program, it should be staffed by a small number of caregivers who spend a lot of time with the babies. There is no way that a group of eight babies can be cared for well by six or eight caregivers, each working part time. At the same time, however, it is unreasonable (although unfortunately common) to expect a caregiver to do a good job caring for babies eight hours a day. Caregivers need scheduled time away from babies if they are to do a good job. This time away can be used to read, do ratings, talk with other staff members, as well as relax. Caregivers should be able to take advantage of naptime or a lull in the activity to have a short break. During the day there will be some shifting of caregivers. This must be accomplished smoothly by having schedules overlap so that there is continuity for the babies and the opportunity for caregivers to exchange information. It is not enough to rely on written information.

One of the problems inherent in infant caregiving is that much of the job may seem very routine and unchanging after the necessary skills have been mastered. Caregivers often lose sight of the impor-

tance and meaningfulness of what they are doing. Unlike working with older children or adults, many of the rewards of working with babies are very subtle, very small. It takes a sensitive person to notice, appreciate, and be gratified by a shaky reach or a baby going to sleep without screaming or stacking two blocks or reaching out for her. These are the rewards of caring for babies, the results of countless sensitive caregiving acts. Caregivers need to be reminded, by being praised, by having the opportunity to teach others the skills they have, by being helped to grow and learn in their profession, that theirs is a very important, highly skilled job.

Chapter 8. Staff Composition, Training, and Morale—Notes

1. Jorn, M.; Persky, B.; and Huntington, D.C. "Selection of Staff." In *The Infants We Care For*, edited by L.L. Dittmann. Washington, D.C.: National Association for the Education of Young Children, 1973.

2. Abt Associates, Inc. *Costs and Quality Issues for Operators*. Washington, D.C.: Day Care and Child Development Council of America, 1972.
Host, M.S., and Heller, P.B. *Day Care 7: Administration*. Washington, D.C.: U.S. Government Printing Office, 1971 [DHEW Publication No. (OCD) 72-20].

3. There are many excellent sources of information available for training caregivers.

Honig, A.S., and Lally, J.R. *Infant Caregiving: A Design for Training.* New York: Media Products, 1972.

Institute for Child Mental Health. *Building Skills for Day Care of Infants.* Monograph 9. New York: Institute for Child Mental Health, 1973.

This report of a training project done in three day care centers in the New York City area is especially valuable for its sensitivity in discussing the difficulties of changing caregivers' attitudes and ideas about babies and their care.

Jorn, M.; Persky, B.; and Keister, M.E. "Training of Staff." In *The Infants We Care For,* edited by L.L. Dittmann. Washington, D.C.: National Association for the Education of Young Children, 1973.

Parker, R.K., and Dittmann, L.L. *Day Care 5: Staff Training.* Washington, D.C.: U.S. Government Printing Office, 1971 [DHEW Publication No. (OCD) 72-23].

4. See Chapter 5, notes 3 and 4, which contain several references dealing with normal infant development and individual differences.

5. Some of the more widely used developmental tests for infants are described in the following.

Bayley, N. *Bayley Scales of Infant Development—Manual.* New York: Psychological Corporation, 1969.

Cattell, P. *The Measurement of Intelligence of Infants and Young Children.* New York: Psychological Corporation, 1940.

Gesell, A., et al. *The First Five Years of Life.* New York: Harper, 1940.

Griffiths, R. *The Abilities of Babies.* New York: McGraw-Hill, 1954.

A more recently developed screening procedure for tentative identification of infants and preschoolers with potential developmental difficulties is described in the following reference.

Frankenburg, W.K.; Goldstein, A.; and Camp, B.W. "The Revised Denver Developmental Screening Test: Its Accuracy as a Screening Instrument." *Journal of Pediatrics* 79 (1971):988-995.

Chapter 9

Physical Space and Equipment

The quality of the social environment in a day care program is more crucial for a good experience for babies than is the elaborateness of the physical setting and equipment. It is quite possible to run an excellent program in much less than ideal physical conditions. However, the arrangement of the rooms in which a day care center is operated, as well as the physical facilities and equipment available, can either facilitate a smooth, pleasant operation or make it more difficult. This does not mean that the more modern the furniture, the more expensive the toys, the plusher the carpet, the better the program will be. A secondhand rocking chair painted bright yellow, carpet remnants, pictures cut from magazines and taped to the wall help create the right atmosphere.

The size of a day care facility, as well as the kinds of space and equipment needed, depend, of course, on the scope of the program and the number of children served. The focus of much of the discussion of physical facilities here is to provide a safe, interesting environment that will encourage exploration and take advantage of the babies' capabilities, whatever they are. The following suggestions are by no means prescriptive, but describe general arrangements which can be adapted to meet the specific needs and limitations of particular situations.[1]*

Room Arrangement

Few people setting up a day care program have the luxury of designing their own facilities. Usually programs are housed in rooms that already exist in churches, schools, industries, or community centers. However, there are a number of definite considerations one needs to keep in mind in designing the floor plan or adapting a group of rooms for use as a center.

There seems to be an inverse relation between apparent room size and infant mobility—that is, as more babies become mobile, the smaller the room seems. It is impossible to prescribe appropriate room size for different numbers of babies, since other factors, such as babies' ages, equipment in the room, arrangement of space, and access to other rooms affect the amount of space needed. Some state regulations prescribe room size in terms of square footage per child.

The following diagram indicates the general size and arrangement of rooms. It is intended primarily to indicate the kinds of rooms needed and their spatial relation to one another.

---

*Footnotes for this chapter are located on page 143.

Rationale for General Layout

Whatever the size and layout of physical space, the arrangement of equipment should be based on functional areas of the program— namely, arrival and departure, feeding, play, sleeping, diapering. A consideration of traffic flow will lead to better organization of space.

It is desirable, if possible, to have a separate sleeping room adjacent to the playroom, so that there is a quiet place for napping. The playroom is the center of action, with all the other rooms leading off from it. An observation booth might extend the length of the sleeping room and playroom (this is a desirable feature, but by no means essential). The bathroom is easily accessible for rinsing dirty diapers and washing hands after each diaper change. The kitchen is close by the playroom and feeding area for easy food preparation. Since the playroom should be equipped with adequate storage areas, a large storage room can be located away from the playroom. It is used as a place to store equipment not currently being used in the room. A multipurpose room used for parent conferences, or working with a single baby, or as a sick room, as well as an office for staff members, should be located a short distance from the main playroom.

SCHEMATIC DRAWING OF A SPATIAL ARRANGEMENT
FOR AN INFANT NURSERY

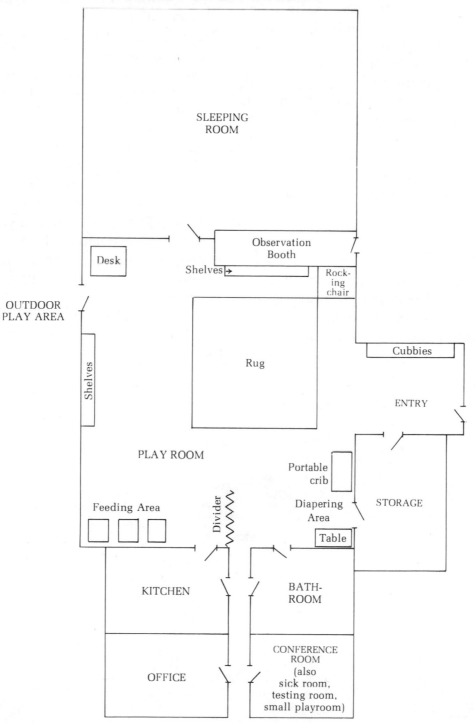

(The spatial arrangement of the Cornell Infant Nursery was similar to that portrayed above insofar as the playroom and sleeping room are concerned. Our arrangements of the adjacent rooms, however, while adequate, were not as convenient and desirable as those suggested in the drawing.)

Entrance

A cubby for each baby in an entryway is a storage place for an extra change of clothes, coats, and other supplies. If the entry is large enough, it should be equipped with table and chairs, so that the parents can undress the baby and get him ready to go home outside the playroom. This cuts down on the confusion at arrival and departure time, or at least centers it away from the playroom.

Playroom

Since it is a multipurpose room, the arrangement of the playroom is important. A good general plan is to set up the room in areas, leaving the rug area as open as possible. Blind spots in the room, places where babies would be completely out of the caregivers' view for long periods of time, should be avoided. Sometimes a baby does need to be away from the rest of the group, however, and the room should be equipped for this, with a large box to crawl into or interesting corners, for example. (A playpen, a feeding table, and the caregiver's lap can also serve this purpose.) The small room away from the playroom can be used when the caregiver can accompany the baby who needs to get away from the group.

In setting up the room, one should think about traffic flow and

arrange the room to minimize confusion. Toy shelves placed just at the edge of the rug allow the baby to crawl over easily to get toys, and the toys will make less noise when they are pulled off the shelf onto the rug. The diapering area could be conveniently situated near the bathroom, the feeding area near the kitchen.

Just inside the entrance to the playroom is a good area to have a bulletin board for parents, a place to keep information on each baby's day.

There should be a desk for the caregivers to keep written records, receive phone calls, to keep current reading material on babies and day care. A telephone in the room will mean that babies will not be left unattended while caregivers take calls. The room should be equipped with comfortable rocking chairs or straight chairs for a caregiver to sit on while feeding, playing with or reading to a baby on her lap, or soothing a baby who is upset or irritable. A clock should be visible from all parts of the room. Besides play equipment, pictures, posters, or perhaps a few mobiles add color to the room.

Shelves for play equipment should be attached to the wall or heavy enough so that they cannot be pulled over. Of course, they should be low enough so that the babies can reach at least some of the toys and choose what they want to play with.

A cabinet storage area close to a changing table near the bathroom will contain supplies such as diapers, blankets, pads, and lotions. This storage area should, of course, be inaccessible to the babies.

Individual feeding tables double as playing tables where a baby can watch what is happening while working with some small toy. There are infant seats for younger babies, and perhaps a windup swing and a walker.

Especially when one room has to accommodate both mobile and nonmobile babies, having some way of dividing the room or sec-

tioning off a portion of it is advantageous. A low fence built in hinged sections and made of a strong but transparent mesh that can fold against the wall when not in use can be used to enclose a safe space on the floor for a younger baby, or to keep the crowds away at feeding time. It should be constructed so that it does not put the babies out of view of the caregivers. Large pillows, especially chairlike pillows with arms, can be helpful to the baby just learning to sit up. Small thermal blankets should be placed on the rug for younger babies, who tend to spit up more than older babies.

A portion of the playroom should be covered with a rug so that the babies can play safely on it. Comfortable floor covering also encourages caregivers to get down on the floor with the babies. As the babies begin to learn to crawl and walk, some padding on the floor will prevent serious head injuries

and some (though by no means all) bumps and bruises. A rug gives better traction for the bare feet or knees of creepers, crawlers, scooters, and walkers than does a tile or wooden floor. Also, some floors tend to be cold during the winter months, and a rug acts as an insulator. The carpeting must be easy to clean and must be tacked down or bound on the edges to keep curious babies from pulling it apart.

Only a part of the floor needs to be carpeted, however. The rest may be tile or another surface that can be cleaned easily. The area of the room where feeding takes place, especially when babies begin to feed themselves, will have to be cleaned daily. Even floor surfaces help the baby learn about the world. For example, a ball goes a long way with a little push on a tile floor, but not on the rug. On the other hand, crawling is easier on the less slippery rug.

The playroom should be spacious, bright, and cheerful. It is desirable for windows to be low

138

enough so that toddlers or even babies who are not yet walking can look out, especially if there are interesting things to look at on the other side. At Cornell the view from the playroom windows, which started about 20 inches away from the floor, was of the nursery school playyard, where there was almost always someone interesting to watch. The windows worked both ways, of course, so the babies were often looked at by the children on the other side. Windows should be made either of shatterproof glass or provided with other kinds of protection, such as wide ledges or screens, to prevent the babies from banging the windows with toys, breaking them, or climbing in them. The windows do not necessarily need to be curtained, especially if the view is nice. A pretty shade or attractive cornice allows natural light to come in. Windows that open and close allow for control of ventilation and temperature if they are screened.

Overhead lights should be sufficient to light the room, but neither glaring nor dull. Lamp fixtures plugged into wall outlets should be used with care to avoid dangerous cords that the babies can chew or pull. Exposed outlets should be covered with protectors.

If radiators are used for heating, they must be enclosed to prevent burns. In maintaining a comfortable room temperature, care-

givers must remember that the warmest air is closer to the ceiling of the room, so if the temperature feels just right to someone standing upright and moving around, it probably means that a baby lying on the floor will be a bit cool.

A portable crib in the room serves several purposes: (1) It provides an area where babies can be diapered without fear of falling or being distracted by other babies; (2) It allows a younger baby to play out of the way of older babies; (3) It gives an older child an area to play without interruption, for instance, on a day when feeling especially irritable and sensitive to interruptions by other babies; (4) It provides a place for a baby to have milk or juice without being bothered.

Two pieces of equipment designed for the Cornell program have helped the caregivers and the babies. A piece of curved pipe bracketed to the wall with a hook at the

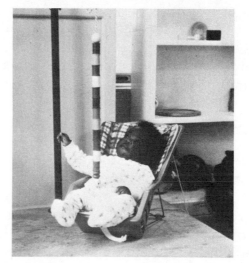

end of it to hang toys from is great for younger babies. They can be strapped into the infant seat and a string of spools, a toy to bat at, or even a teddy bear can be suspended at arm level.

The other piece of equipment is a small, low table about 14 inches high, which the babies use to place small toys on, climb on, and sit on. A slightly raised edge on the table surface keeps toys from falling off so easily. Some of these tables also were built to put toys at arm level for young babies in an infant seat.

It is very easy even in a small program for the playroom to become cluttered. This can be avoided to some extent by making a conscious effort to put away equipment that is not being used.

Kitchen

A kitchen located next to the playroom allows for easy assembling of foods, warming bottles, and cleanup near the end of the day. State regulations may be quite specific about kitchen facilities. Counter space or a table is necessary for putting together food trays and for placing the sterilizer within easy reach. Storage space in the kitchen would be used for food and frequently used utensils. A tiled floor in the kitchen is maintained easily. A refrigerator is used for storing bottles of milk and formula, leftover baby foods, teething rings, and medicines. In any all-day program for infants and toddlers, a stove is necessary for sterilizing eating equipment and warming bottles, as well as preparing hot lunches. The use of a dishwasher will eliminate the need for sterilization.

A half door between the kitchen and the playroom, as well as between the entry and playroom, will allow the caregivers to check on babies easily.

Sleeping Room

Although the sleeping room or area should be pleasant, it should be a serene room more than a bright one. The room should be spacious, so that cribs are not close together. A rug on the floor will help keep noise at a minimum. A fan securely mounted high on the wall out of the babies' reach serves a dual purpose: it increases air circulation and provides a quiet noise to mask other noises in the room. Windows should be shaded so that the amount of light in the room can be regulated. A rocking chair in the sleeping room can be used by caregivers to help babies go to sleep, to calm them, or help them relax away from the color, noise, and activity of the playroom. There should be a storage area in the sleeping room for bed linens, a few crib toys, and materials for diaper changes.

Each baby should have his or her own crib to sleep in regularly, and those babies having similar sleeping patterns should be in the same part of the room. Cribs should be situated away from windows and wall sockets. Cotton sheets and blankets cut down on static electricity and are durable. There should not be pillows in the cribs. There are several points to be made about cribs: The mattresses should be easy to clean; it must be possible to lower mattresses so that babies cannot climb or fall over the sides; they should of course be safely and sturdily constructed, and should allow the baby to see out into the room. Cribs should have slats that are no more than 2⅜ inches apart, rails at least 26 inches high, locks and latches secure from accidental release, and hardware with smooth edges. Soft music is calming for some babies, so a radio or record player in the sleeping room as well as in the playroom might make naptime easier for caregiver and baby.

Other Rooms

The bathroom should be large enough to hold diaper pails. A lockable cabinet in this room can be used to keep medication, wash cloths, and cleaning materials close at hand. A storage room can accommodate a washer and dryer (a must for a program unless they use

141

a diaper service), extra supplies and equipment not currently in use. The extra multipurpose room should be equipped with a crib for a sick baby. Other equipment will be determined by the use of the room. An office away from the nursery is essential for staff members. It should contain a place for storing information as well as a work space. An observation booth is perhaps an unreasonable suggestion for a non-experimental nursery; however, it is indispensable as a tool for training caregivers through observation and accommodating visitors and parents without disrupting the program.

142

Small equipment, for example, toys and feeding dishes, have not been covered in this section. Other sections of the book (feeding and play time) contain information about this equipment.

Playyard

If possible, an outside play area provides for the important experience of getting out and going to a new place, preferably out of doors. Some centers may not have such an area just outside the door, but perhaps arrangements could be made to take the babies to a nearby suitable spot.

Chapter 9. Physical Space and Equipment—Notes

1. Evans, E.B., and Saia, G.E. *Day Care for Infants*. Boston: Beacon Press, 1972.

Sale, J. *Programs for Infants and Young Children. Part IV: Facilities and Equipment.* Washington, D.C.: Appalachian Regional Commission, 1970.

Chapter 10

Health and Safety

A clean, safe, healthy environment is a necessary background for providing good experiences for babies. Many of the concerns in the areas of health and safety that are relevant to parents caring for a baby at home apply to the operation of a day care center as well. Much of the discussion of specific issues relating to health and safety, e.g., feeding, diapering, play, physical space and equipment, occurs in other chapters. This chapter will highlight briefly some general guidelines for maintaining optimal health and safety conditions. The chapter is intended to be a starting point for learning about an area where caregivers need to be very knowledgeable. Many state and federal guidelines pertain to the issues of health and safety in day care centers and are good sources to consult for minimum guidelines.[1]*

The general guidelines in this chapter fall into three main categories: policy on illnesses, routines to ensure good health, and safety concerns.

Policy on Babies' Illnesses

First, of course, caregivers must be in good health and have periodic checkups to ensure this. They should stay away from the babies if they have fresh colds, per-

_____
*Footnotes for this chapter are located on page 151.

sistent coughs, other respiratory infections—in short, anything that a baby could catch.

Every program must work out its own policy in accordance with state regulations regarding illness—when babies can be with the group and when they should not be with other babies. This policy should be explained very carefully to parents at the outset in order to prevent misunderstandings later.

The policy for caring for moderately sick babies in the center will be partially determined by staff and facilities available—that is, whether or not a sick baby can be cared for without endangering the health of the other babies. Obviously, very sick infants cannot be cared for in the average day care center. In recent years, however, there has been a trend toward trying to care for mildly ill babies in centers rather than excluding them. A baby with an infectious illness must be cared for in a place somewhat apart from other babies, and therefore requires some special attention by one caregiver. By way of illustration, the guidelines given to parents of babies in the Cornell Nursery are presented in Appendix G. Babies with temperatures over 101° should not be in with other babies, since this is a symptom of a major infection that could spread. No baby with moderate or severe diarrhea should stay in the nursery. This is highly contagious. Eye infections such as conjunctivitis spread easily, so a baby with this should be kept out until it is under control. On the other hand, it is common for babies to have mild colds during much of the winter, so sneezes, runny noses, and mild coughs are not sufficient reasons for isolation or exclusion. In the same way, a baby who has been out with a cold or respiratory infection does not have to stay away until the symptoms have completely disappeared. Each program will have to settle on its own guidelines with the help of health specialists such as pediatricians or pediatric nurses, and enforce them consistently.

As mentioned in the outline of necessary staff responsibilities (Chapter 8), each day care center should have ready access to a nurse or other person well trained in matters relating to health and illnesses, or to a health resource that can give practical advice. Caregivers should be knowledgeable about common illnesses in babies and symptoms to look for.[2] A list of symptoms and illnesses that warrant calling a physician is given in Appendix H. Caregivers should be informed about any medication the baby is receiving at home or in the nursery—what the medication is for, when it should be given to the baby, and possible side effects. For the protection of the staff as well as the babies, caregivers should give medication of any kind (including aspirin or vitamins) to babies only when they have written permission from parents. Daily information from the parents on the baby's general health will aid the caregivers in meeting the baby's needs. Caregivers can also be a valuable source of health information to the parents. It should be a requirement of the program that the baby have all immunizations up to date and that each child has regular checkup visits with a pediatrician, whether through the parents or the center.

Routines to Ensure Good Health

There are many practices which, if they become an integral part of the routine, will establish a healthy setting for children and adults. Some recommendations are:

1. Daily vacuuming of the floor, especially in the feeding area, or cleaning up spills and damp mopping every other day is usually sufficient.

2. Daily or more frequent cleaning of most frequently used equipment such as infant seats, feeding tables, diapering tables. Diapering tables can be covered with paper or cloth.

3. Periodic cleaning of all equipment and daily washing of toys and play equipment which become sticky.

4. Putting a washable blanket on the floor under younger babies who are likely to spit up to avoid soiling the rug, and washing the blanket frequently.

5. Changing diapers when wet or soiled.

6. Carefully cleaning the baby during diaper changes and using a good skin care technique to prevent diaper rashes (p. 101).

7. Caregivers washing hands before and after each diapering.

8. Sterilizing or washing bottles in a dishwasher for

147

young babies and careful washing of eating utensils.

9. Keeping bottles out of the refrigerator for no more than thirty or forty minutes, unless they are prepackaged.

10. Washing babies' hands before and after feeding when finger feeding begins.

11. Changing babies' clothes if they become wet or very soiled during the day.

12. Changing each baby's bed linens at least once a week or more frequently if they become soiled.

Safety

The day care setting where a baby spends much time should be "baby-proof"—that is, a place without excessive prohibitions, where the baby is free to explore and the caregivers do not have to be constantly concerned about potentially dangerous situations in the room.

One of the most effective general guidelines for ensuring such a safe setting for babies is that caregivers should set up the room and carry out the day's activities with the assumption that all babies are capable of doing a lot more than one might expect on the basis of their age. A caregiver should never feel sure, for example, that a three- or four-month-old cannot roll over or wriggle off a surface, that an eight-month-old would not try to pull up to standing by a wobbly table, that an eleven-month-old would not try to climb out of the feeding table, or that a twelve-month-old would not be interested in stretching to reach a drinking glass sitting on a table. It is best to assume that a baby will do all the things he or she is capable of—and more!

A good many safety concerns have to do with the physical arrangements and facilities.

1. There should be no hanging electrical or drapery cords to be pulled on, tripped over, or chewed.

2. Electrical outlets within the babies' reach must be covered with safety plug outlets or concealed behind stationary furniture.

3. There should be no slippery throw rugs in the room. Caregivers should wear shoes that give them a firm footing when they are carrying babies. Walking babies also should not wear slippery shoes.

4. Highly flammable fabrics and fiberglass should not be used in draperies, for instance.

148

5. The room should be planned for easy exit in case of fire or other emergencies. Practice fire drills to carry out a plan for moving all the babies outside will make the job easier in case of a real emergency. The room should be equipped with fire extinguishers and a fire blanket.

6. Windows and mirrors should be made of shatterproof glass or protected by wide ledges or screens (see p. 139).

7. Radiators or floor heaters must be covered.

8. Some house plants are poisonous if the foilage or fruit is chewed. A room where babies are is no place for such plants. Any other plants should be hung or placed above the children's reach to guard against spilled soil or broken pots.

9. Unstable furniture, for instance shelves, that a baby might tip over on himself or herself does not belong in a nursery.

10. Crib mattresses should be lowered long before it seems likely that a baby could jump or fall over the sides of the crib.

In even the safest physical setting, the welfare of the children depends primarily on the attentiveness of conscientious caregivers. The following list of responsibilities should become a natural part of the caregiver's role.

1. Pick up small play materials which might trip adults or babies.

2. Keep supplies such as medicine, cleaning materials, and plastic bags in a place that is locked. They must be absolutely inaccessible to babies; do not leave them out for even a short time.

3. Check equipment often for loose pieces, swallowable parts, sharp edges, breakability.

4. Be aware of equipment that is designed for use only when a caregiver is attending the baby—for example, a long string or rope, a drumstick or long wooden spoon for pounding, aluminum foil to crinkle, climbing equipment. Store them out of children's reach, and use them appropriately.

5. Be sure hands are dry when handling baby, to ensure a firm grip.

6. Place the young baby in a sitting position (or near sitting) while he is eating or getting a bottle to prevent choking. **Never** prop a bottle for a baby who cannot hold it himself or herself.

7. Keep babies' nails trimmed so they will not scratch themselves or other people.

8. Do not put objects—cups of hot coffee, for instance—near the edge of a desk or table or on a towel or diaper that a baby could pull down on himself or herself.

9. Use only plastic bottles (no glass ones) when babies begin holding their bottles. A broken bottle is very difficult to clean up thoroughly enough to make the floor safe again for crawlers.

10. Keep informed about proper first aid practices.

11. Keep a list near the telephone of emergency numbers, plus the numbers for all parents and their pediatricians.

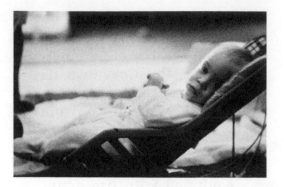

12. Use infant seats only for very young babies who cannot tip them over.

13. Place heavier equipment on lower toy shelves. If the babies have to reach up, they are apt to pull such items down on themselves.

14. Be aware of what mobile babies are doing and help them stay out of dangerous situations that occur when their courage exceeds their skills (in climbing into chairs or standing on low furniture, for example).

15. Be very watchful of mobile babies who may, in their interest in exploring, hurt another baby. Be especially protective of nonmobile babies, who do not have the option of moving away.

16. Use rocking chairs cautiously when crawlers are moving about.

150

In reality, no setting or program is truly "baby-proof" and the well-being of the children is dependent on the alertness and attentiveness of well-trained staff operating in a setting where hazards are at a minimum.

Chapter 10. Health and Safety—Notes

1. American Academy of Pediatrics. *Standards for Day Care Centers for Infants and Children Under 3 Years of Age.* Evanston, Ill.: American Academy of Pediatrics, 1971. Also available from Day Care and Child Development Council of America, 1401 K St., N.W., Washington, D.C. 20005.

North, A.F. *Day Care 6: Health Services.* Washington, D.C.: U.S. Government Printing Office, 1971 [DHEW Publication No. (OCD) 72-4].

2. Spock, B. *Baby and Child Care.* New York: Pocket Books, 1970.

Vaughan, G. *Mummy, I Don't Feel Well: a Pictorial Guide to Common Childhood Illnesses.* London: Berkeley Graphics, 1970.

Chapter 11

Epilogue

If this book has accomplished the purpose the authors intend it to serve, then three things should have happened to the person who has studied it: (1) He or she is firmly convinced that caring for infants in a group setting is an exciting, pleasurable, challenging, and complex job; (2) The value of guidelines to provide a rationale for caregiving practices has been established; (3) As many questions and issues have been raised as there have been answers given. The book should be seen not as a "how-to-do-it" book but rather as a beginning point for creative caregiving.

The issue of day care, particularly day care for infants, carries with it many unresolved questions and areas of concern for parents, for people involved directly in operating programs, and for those people whose interests lie in areas related

to day care—child development, nutrition, job training, community organization, policy formulation, and political processes, to mention a few. In the paragraphs which follow, we discuss briefly five issues of major concern to anyone involved in any capacity with group care for infants and young children. These issues, some of which have been raised in previous chapters, must be confronted in further efforts to ensure quality group care.

Status of Caregiving as a Profession

Much was said in Chapter 8, "Staff Composition, Training, and Morale," to imply that programs are better when caregivers see themselves as highly skilled professionals doing a very rewarding but difficult job. However, it will be impossible for them to maintain that attitude unless it is shared by other staff members, parents, and society in general. Increased recognition and valuing of competent caregiving, whether by mothers, fathers, or caregivers outside the home, is very likely to lead to an upgrading of the quality of the experience young children have in group care settings, especially if the valuing is reflected in the salaries caregivers receive and in the status they are accorded. Higher salaries would also attract a wider variety of skilled people to jobs in day care.

There is a more serious issue related to the status of caregivers: Can bright competent people be motivated to *continue* working as caregivers? Those people who actually care for the children have the most important jobs in day care, and yet often highly skilled caregivers move away quite soon from the children into administrative or supervisory positions. Two characteristics of caring for babies contribute to a lack of challenge and excitement in the job. First, much time is spent doing the same things over and over. Secondly, the rewards are often subtle and meaningful primarily to those people who have been trained and are sensitized to babies' development and behavior. In summary, caregiving may sometimes seem boring, and the authors want to raise this issue for consideration, particularly by those people operating centers and working with caregivers. They must be aware of the possibility of boredom and do all they can to ensure that caregiving is a fulfilling experience for those people who have the skills, the sensitivity, and the motivation to do it best.

Maintaining Program Quality

Once quality has been achieved in caregiving practices and overall program operation, an active effort to maintain that quality must be pursued. Very often, providing the best experience possible for each baby—making pleasurable learning situations out of routine caregiving, for instance—demands more of the caregiver than does just coping, meeting daily needs, and doing an adequate job. There must be something within the program that continuously makes it worthwhile for caregivers to put forth the extra effort to care for babies in the best way they know how. This incentive must be more than some kind of periodic evaluation, although this may help. In Chapter 8 we discussed the importance of keeping caregivers enthusiastic about their work and eager to improve. Supporting this kind of attitude, combined with a more structured internal periodic assessment or review of the program, can best ensure program quality.

Variety of Programs

No single program or general approach to caregiving is going to be best for all babies and families, just as no one set of guidelines and advice on childrearing is likely to work successfully with all children. The authors see the guidelines in this book as being applicable to a relatively wide range of programs and settings. However, just as the emphasis in this book is on tailoring caregiving to meet the needs of individual babies served, so programs should be designed to offer families a choice among different child-care situations. Every program will be unique, partly be-

cause of individual constraints on physical space, budgeting, size and age range of the group of children. This is desirable since different kinds of programs are best for different families and babies. For example, the typically smaller family day care group might be better for some babies than a larger group care setting. Some parents may prefer to have their young children cared for close to where they are working, while others may prefer a location in the neighborhood where they live, such as a family day care home.[1]*

Cost of Day Care

Quality day care is expensive, and the cost will be higher as programs are tailored to meet the varying needs of different families and children. The high cost of quality day care is a complex problem for which there is no simple solution. Reducing costs is difficult without compromising the quality of the care. Using local resources, both money as well as manpower and skills, may bring down some of the costs. However, the best solution is for society to value quality child care, accept the fact that it is both expensive and needed, and support it financially through appropriate legislative action.

---

*Footnotes for this chapter are located on pages 157-158.

Effects of Day Care

One of the most critical questions people ask about day care is "What are its effects on the infant's development, parent-infant relationships, and relationships within the family generally?" In other words, is it good for infants to spend a substantial amount of time in day care? Of course, this question is of more practical relevance for parents who have a clear choice in the matter, for whom infant day care is in no sense a necessity, than for those families in which, for financial or other reasons, some infant care outside the home is necessary.

Those parents who have a choice sometimes wonder if it might be better for their infant to spend some time in day care, rather than being reared entirely at home, as a way of broadening experience and furthering development. Or, some mothers who have a strong desire to continue working outside the home after the birth of a child ask if both they and their baby might not be better off, and might not have a better relationship, if the mother's wish to be employed can be fulfilled by having the infant cared for outside the home at least part of the time. There are no easy definitive general answers to these questions, and parents have to answer them pretty much for themselves, based on their own values and feelings, and with a careful consideration of the alternatives that are open to them, particularly the quality of group care available.

For the many families in which for economic or other reasons infant day care is a necessity, one of society's concerns should be to ensure that this group care is of the highest quality, and that it is oriented toward strengthening families and their care of their young children.

Our own view is that a variety of ways of caring for infants ought to be available to *all* families, regardless of economic or other circumstances. Such options should include more broadly available resources for providing good care outside the home when this is desired. At the same time, however, we believe it is important to stress the value of good home care by parents, especially during the first few years of life. This important option should be open also to families under economic duress, if necessary through the provision of appropriate financial support.

It is our opinion that while experience in a quality group care setting *may* provide some opportunities for learning and development which may not be as easily available at home, a good home environment can be entirely adequate for promoting healthy development in the first three years of life. Good full-time care of a baby by

156

parents should be viewed, then, not as less desirable than group care or as one option among many, but rather as a particularly valuable and desirable beginning for babies and young children.

As mentioned in the introductory chapter, there is still much to be learned about the effects of extensive experience in group care settings outside the home upon the infant and the family. These effects are quite difficult to assess precisely for a variety of technical reasons. In addition, carrying out and interpreting the results of studies of the consequences of day care early in life in a neutral and objective manner is made more difficult because there tend to be such strong feelings *for* or *against* day care in our society generally, and to some extent even among specialists in child development. These feelings are based in part upon strongly held political, social, or value orientations toward day care and family life. In this atmosphere, even very tentative research findings suggesting possibly advantageous or disadvantageous effects of group care outside the home in the first year of life tend to be seized upon somewhat prematurely as evidence for or against some social or political point of view already held.

We believe that it is very important for parents as well as policy makers and planners to maintain a calm and openminded orientation toward these issues, and to avoid doctrinaire points of view and simplistic answers supporting them. At the same time, we need to continue to seek ways of ensuring the best possible care for infants both at home as well as outside the home, and to continue to study the effects of different arrangements for providing infant care as a basis for wiser planning. It is to these ends that our book and modest research efforts have been addressed.

In closing, we would like to re-emphasize the importance of day care programs as supplements to and reinforcers of families. Caregivers who view themselves as *working with* parents *rather than substituting for* them can play a crucial role not only in enhancing the baby's development but also in strengthening the entire family.

Chapter 11. Epilogue—Notes

1. Lists and descriptions of various kinds of programs for infants are contained in the following publications.

Howard, M. "Group Infant Care Programs, a Survey." Washington, D.C.: Consortium on Early Childbearing and Childrearing, 1971.

Appalachian Regional Commission. *Programs for Infants and Young Children. Part 1. Education and Day Care.* Washington, D.C.: Appalachian Regional Commission, 1970.

Huntington, D.S.; Provence, S.; and Parker, R.K. *Day Care 2: Serving Infants.* Washington, D.C.: U.S. Government Printing Office, 1971 [DHEW Publication No. (OCD) 72-8].

Below are some organizations with written materials on topics of concern to those involved in infant programs.

Association for Childhood Education International, 3615 Wisconsin Avenue, N.W., Washington, D.C. 20016

Child Welfare League of America, Inc., 67 Irving Place, New York, N.Y. 10003

Consortium on Early Childbearing and Childrearing. Publications are available through the Child Welfare League of America, 67 Irving Place, New York, NY.
A publication of interest from the Consortium is: Williams, T.M. *Infant Care: Abstracts of the Literature.*

Day Care and Child Development Council of America, Inc., 1401 K Street, N.W., Washington, D.C. 20005

North Carolina Training Center for Infant-Toddler Care, University of North Carolina at Greensboro, Greensboro, NC 27412

National Association for the Education of Young Children, 1834 Connecticut Ave., N.W., Washington, D.C. 20009

Alphabetic List of References Included in Chapter Notes

ABT Associates, Inc. *Costs and Quality Issues for Operators.* Washington, D.C.: Day Care and Child Development Council of America, 1972.

Ainsworth, M.D.S. "The Development of Infant-Mother Attachment." In *Review of Child Development Research, Vol. 3. Child Development and Social Policy,* edited by B.M. Caldwell and H.N. Ricciuti. Chicago: University of Chicago Press, 1973.

American Academy of Pediatrics. *Standards for Day Care Centers for Infants and Children Under 3 Years of Age.* Evanston, Ill.: American Academy of Pediatrics, 1971. Also available from Day Care and Child Development Council of America, 1401 K St., NW, Washington, D.C. 20005.

Appalachian Regional Commission. *Programs for Infants and Young Children.* Washington, D.C.: Appalachian Regional Commission, 1970.
> *Part I: Education and Day Care*
> *Part II: Nutrition*
> *Part III: Health*
> *Part IV: Equipment and Facilities*

Bayley, N. *Bayley Scales of Infant Development—Manual.* New York: Psychological Corporation, 1969.

Bell, S.M., and Ainsworth, M.D.S. "Infant Crying and Maternal Responsiveness." *Child Development* 43 (1972): 1171-1190.

Blehar, M.P. "Anxious Attachment and Defensive Reactions Associated with Day Care." *Child Development* 45 (1974): 683-692

Bogart, L.J.; Briggs, G.M.; and Calloway, D.H. *Nutrition and Physical Fitness.* Philadelphia: W.B. Saunders, 1973.

Bowlby, J. *Attachment and Loss. Vol. 2: Separation.* London: Hogarth, 1973.

Brazelton, T.B. "Working with the Family." In *The Infants We Care For,* edited by L.L. Dittmann. Washington, D.C.: National Association for the Education of Young Children, 1973.

Brazelton, T.B. *Infants and Mothers.* New York: Delacorte Press, 1969.

Breckenridge, M.E., and Murphy, M.N. *Growth and Development of the Young Child,* 8th ed. Philadelphia: W.B. Saunders, 1969.

Bronfenbrenner, U. "When is Infant Stimulation Effective?" In *Environmental Influences,* edited by D.C. Glass. New York: Rockefeller Press and Russell Sage Foundation, 1968.

Caldwell, B.M. "What is the Optimal Learning Environment for the Young Child?" *American Journal of Orthopsychiatry* 37 (1967):8-21.

Caldwell, B.M. "What Does Research Teach Us about Day Care for Children under Three?" *Children Today* 1 (1972): 6-11.

Caldwell, B.M.; Wright, C.M.; Honig, A.S.; and Tannenbaum, J. "Infant Day Care and Attachment." *American Journal of Orthopsychiatry* 40 (1970):397-412.

Cattell, P. *The Measurement of Intelligence of Infants and Young Children.* New York: Psychological Corporation, 1940.

Chandler, C.A.; Lourie, R.S.; and Peters, A.D., eds. *Early Child Care.* New York: Atherton Press, 1968.

Church, J. *Three Babies: Biographies of Cognitive Development.* New York: Random House, 1966.

Cohlan, S.Q. *Baby Care: a Program for Self-Instruction.* New York: Instructional Materials Laboratories, 1970.

Conserco, Inc. *Child Care Bulletin No. 4, subject: A Survey of State Day Care Licensing Requirements.* Washington, D.C.: Day Care and Child Development Council of America, 1972.

Day Care Council of New York. *So You're Going to Run a Day Care Service.* New York: Day Care Council of New York, 1971.

Department of Health, Education, and Welfare. *The Federal Interagency Day Care Requirements of 1968.* Reprinted by the Day Care and Child Development Council of America, Washington, D.C.

Department of Health, Education, and Welfare; Maternal and Child Health Service. *Nutrition and Feeding of Infants and Children Under Three in Group Day Care.* Washington, D.C.: U.S. Government Printing Office, 1971 [DHEW Publication No. (HM) 72-5606].

Dittmann, L.L., ed. *The Infants We Care For.* Washington, D.C.: National Association for the Education of Young Children, 1973.

Durfee, J.T., and Lee, L.C. "Infant-Infant Interaction in Day Care Setting." Paper presented at meetings of American Psychological Association, August 1973, Montreal, Canada, (Technical Report, Cornell Research Program in Early Development and Education. Ithaca, N.Y.: Cornell University, August 1973.).

Etzel, B.C., and Gewirtz, J.L. "Experimental Modification of Caretaker-Maintained High-Rate Operant Crying in a 6- and 20-week Old Infant: Extinction of Crying with Reinforcement of Eye Contact and Smiling." *Journal of Experimental Child Psychology* 5 (1967):303-307.

Evans, E.B., and Saia, G.E. *Day Care for Infants.* Boston: Beacon Press, 1972.

Evans, E.B.; Shub, B.; and Weinstein, M. *Day Care.* Boston: Beacon Press, 1971.

Fein, G.G., and Clarke-Stewart, A. *Day Care in Context.* New York: John Wiley & Sons, 1973.

Fowler, W. "The Effect of Early Stimulation: the Problem of Focus in Developmental Stimulation." *Merrill-Palmer Quarterly* 15 (1969):159-170.

Fowler, W. "A Developmental Learning Approach to Infant Care in a Group Setting." *Merrill-Palmer Quarterly* 18 (1972): 145-175.

Fowler, W., and Biderman, E. *Developmental Methods for Physical Care Routines with Infants.* Toronto, Ontario:

162

Ontario Institute for Studies in Education, 1972.

Frankenburg, W.K.; Goldstein, A.; and Camp, B.W. "The Revised Denver Developmental Screening Test: Its Accuracy as a Screening Instrument." *Journal of Pediatrics* 79 (1971):988-995.

Gesell, A., et al. *The First Five Years of Life.* New York: Harper, 1940.

Gordon, I.J. *Baby Learning through Baby Play.* New York: St. Martin's Press, 1970.

Granato, S., and Krone, E. *Day Care 8: Serving Children with Special Needs.* Washington, D.C.: U.S. Government Printing Office, 1972 [DHEW Publication No. (OCD) 72-42].

Griffiths, R. *The Abilities of Babies.* New York: McGraw-Hill, 1954.

Grotberg, E.H., ed. *Day Care: Resources for Decisions.* Washington, D.C.: Office of Economic Opportunity, 1971.

Honig, A.S., and Lally, R.J. *Infant Caregiving: A Design for Training.* New York: Media Press, 1972.

Horowitz, F.D., and Paden, L.Y. "The Effectiveness of Environmental Intervention Programs." In *Review of Child Development Research, Vol. 3: Child Development and Social Policy,* edited by B.M. Caldwell and H.N. Ricciuti. Chicago: University of Chicago Press, 1973.

Host, M.S., and Heller, P.B. *Day Care 7: Administration.* Washington, D.C.: U.S. Government Printing Office, 1971 [DHEW Publication No. (OCD) 72-20].

Howard, M. *Group Infant Care Programs, a Survey.* Washington, D.C.: Consortium on early Childbearing and Childrearing, 1971.

Hunt, J. McV. *Intelligence and Experience.* New York: Ronald Press, 1961.

Hunt, J. McV. "The Epigenesis of Intrinsic Motivation and the Fostering of Early Cognitive Development." In *Current Research in Motivation,* edited by R.N. Haber. New York: Holt, Rinehart, and Winston, 1966. Also in Hunt, J. McV. "The

Challenge of Incompetence and Poverty." Urbana, Ill.: University of Illinois Press, 1969.

Huntington, D.S.; Provence, S.; and Parker, R.K. *Day Care 2: Serving Infants.* Washington, D.C.: U.S. Government Printing Office, 1971 [DHEW Publication No. (OCD) 72-8].

Institute for Child Mental Health. *Building Skills for Day Care of Infants.* Monograph 9. New York: Institute for Child Mental Health, 1973.

Johnson, J.E. "Crying and the Relief of Distress in an Infant Day Care Nursery." Technical Report, Cornell Research Program in Early Development and Education. Ithaca, N.Y.: Cornell University, January 1974.

Jorn, M.; Persky, B.; and Huntington, D.S. "Selection of Staff." In *The Infants We Care For,* edited by L.L. Dittmann. Washington, D.C.: National Association for the Education of Young Children, 1973.

Jorn, M.; Persky, B.; and Keister, M.E. "Training of Staff." In *The Infants We Care For,* edited by L.L. Dittmann. Washington, D.C.: National Association for the Education of Young Children, 1973.

Keister, M.E. *"The Good Life" for Infants and Toddlers.* Washington, D.C.: National Association for the Education of Young Children, 1970.

Keister, M.E. "Practical Considerations in the Operation of a Center for Infants and Toddlers and Their Families." In *The Infants We Care For,* edited by L.L. Dittmann. Washington, D.C.: National Association for the Education of Young Children, 1973.

Keister, M.E. *Discipline: the Secret Heart of Child Care.* Greensboro, N.C.: North Carolina Training Center for Infant-Toddler Care, 1973.

Lally, J.R. "Development of a Day Care Center for Young Children." Progress Report of the Syracuse, N.Y. Children's Center, 1969-70.

Lambie, D.Z., and Weikart, D.B. "Ypsilanti-Carnegie Infant Education Project." In *Disadvantaged Child. Vol. III*, edited by J. Hellmuth. New York: Bruner/Mazel, 1970.

Lee, L.C. "Social Encounters of Infants: the Beginnings of Popularity." Paper presented at meetings of the International Society for the Study of Behavioral Development, August 1973, Ann Arbor, MI. (Technical Report, Cornell Research Program in Early Development and Education. Ithaca, N.Y.: Cornell University, August 1973).

Lewis, M., and Wilson, C.D. "Infant Development in Lower Class American Families." *Human Development* 15 (1972):112-127.

Murphy, L.B. "Spontaneous Ways of Learning in Young Children." *Children* 14 (1967):210-216.

Murphy, L.B. "Multiple Factors in Learning in the Day Care Center." *Childhood Education* 45 (1969):311-320.

North, A.F. *Day Care 6: Health Services.* Washington, D.C.: U.S. Government Printing Office, 1971 [DHEW Publication No. (OCD) 72-4].

Office of Child Development, U.S. Department of Health, Education, and Welfare. *Day Care.* Washington, D.C.: U.S. Government Printing Office.

1. *A Statement of Principles,* 1971 [DHEW Publication No. (OCD) 72-10].
2. *Serving Infants,* 1971 [DHEW Publication No. (OCD) 72-8].
3. *Serving Preschool Children,* 1974 [DHEW Publication No. (OCD) 74-1057].
4. *Serving School Age Children,* 1972 [DHEW Publication No. (OCD) 72-34].
5. *Staff Training,* 1971 [DHEW Publication No. (OCD) 72-23].
6. *Health Services,* 1971 [DHEW Publication No. (OCD) 72-4].
7. *Administration,* 1971 [DHEW Publication No. (OCD) 72-20].
8. *Serving Children with Special Needs,* 1972 [DHEW Publication No. (OCD) 72-42].

Office of Child Development, U.S. Department of Health, Education, and Welfare. *Infant Care.* Washington, D.C.: U.S. Government Printing Office, 1972 [DHEW Publication No. (OCD) 73-15, see pp. 17-19].

Office of Child Development, U.S. Department of Health, Education, and Welfare. *Guide for Family Day Care Licensing.* Washington, D.C.: Office of Child Development, U.S. Department of Health, Education, and Welfare, 1973.

Painter, G. "The Effect of a Structured Tutorial Program on the Cognitive and Language Development of Culturally Disadvantaged Infants." *Merrill-Palmer Quarterly* 15 (1969):279-294.

Painter, G. *Teach Your Baby.* New York: Simon & Schuster, 1971.

Parker, R.K., and Dittmann, L.L. *Day Care 5: Staff Training.* Washington, D.C.: U.S. Government Printing Office, 1971 [DHEW Publication No. (OCD) 72-23].

Pechman, S.M. "Seven Parent and Child Centers." *Children Today* 1 (1972):28-31.

Pekarsky, D.; Kagan, J.; and Kearsley, R. *Manual for Infant Development.* No publisher given. Author's address: Dr. Jerome Kagan, Department of Social Relations, Harvard University, Cambridge, Mass. 02138.

Provence, S. *Guide for the Care of Infants in Groups.* New York: Child Welfare League of America, 1971.

Provence, S., and Lipton, R.C. *Infants in Institutions.* New York: International Universities Press, 1962.

Ricciuti, H.N. "Fear and the Development of Social Attachment in the First Year of Life." In *Origins of Human Behavior: Fear,* edited by M. Lewis and L. Rosenblum. New York: John Wiley, 1974.

Ricciuti, H.N., and Poresky, R.H. "Development of Attachment to Caregivers in an Infant Nursery during the First Year of Life." Paper presented at meetings of the Society for Research in Child Development, March 1973, Philadelphia, Pa.

Rutter, M. *Maternal Deprivation Reassessed*. Baltimore: Penguin Books, 1972.

Ryan Jones Associates, Inc. *How to Operate Your Day Care Program*. Wyomissing, Pa.: Ryan Jones Associates, 1970.

Sale, J. *Programs for Infants and Young Children. Part IV: Facilities and Equipment*. Washington, D.C.: Appalachian Regional Commission, 1970.

Saunders, M.M. *The ABC's of Learning in Infancy*. Greensboro, N.C.: University of North Carolina Demonstration Project, 1971.

Spock, B. *Baby and Child Care*. New York: Pocket Books, 1970.

Starr, H. "Cognitive Development in Infancy: Assessment Acceleration, and Actualization." *Merrill-Palmer Quarterly* 17 (1971): 153-186.

Stone, L.J., and Church, J. *Childhood and Adolescence* 3rd ed. New York: Random House, 1973.

Sutton-Smith, B. *Child Psychology*. New York: Appleton-Century-Crofts, 1973.

Tronick, E., and Greenfield, P.M. *Infant Curriculum*. New York: Media Projects, 1973.

Upchurch, B. *Easy-to-do Toys and Activities for Infants and Toddlers*. Available from the Infant Care Project, The University of North Carolina at Greensboro, Greensboro, North Carolina 27412.

Vaughan, G. *Mummy, I Don't Feel Well: A Pictorial Guide to Common Childhood Illnesses*. London: Berkeley Graphics, 1970.

Weikart, D.P., and Lambie, D.Z. "Early Enrichment in Infants." In *Education of the Infant and Young Child*, edited by V.H. Denenberg. New York: Academic Press, 1970.

White, B.L. "Our Goals for the Infant and His Family." In *The Infants We Care For*, edited by L.L. Dittmann. Washington, D.C.: National Association for the Education of Young Children, 1973.

White, B.L., and Watts, J.C. *Experience and Environment. Vol. 1*. Englewood Cliffs, N.J.: Prentice-Hall, 1973.

Williams, T.M. *Infant Care: Abstracts of the Literature*. Washington, D.C.: Consortium on Early Childbearing and Childrearing, Suite 618, 1145 Nineteenth St., N.W., Washington, D.C. 20036 (Child Welfare League of America)

Willis, A., and Ricciuti, H.N. "Longitudinal Observations of Infants' Daily Arrivals at a Day Care Center." Technical Report, Cornell Research Program in Early Development and Education. Ithaca, N.Y.: Cornell University, January 1974.

Work, H.H. "Parent-Child Centers: A Working Reappraisal." *American Journal of Orthopsychiatry* 42 (1972):582-595.

Yarrow, L.J. "Separation from Parents During Early Childhood." In *Review of Child Development Research, Vol. 1*, edited by M.L. Hoffman and L.W. Hoffman. New York: Russell Sage, 1964.

Yarrow, L.J. "Conceptualizing the Early Environment." In *Early Child Care*, edited by C.A. Chandler, R.S. Lourie, and A.D. Peters. New York: Atherton Press, 1968.

Yarrow, L.J.; Rubinstein, J.L.; Pedersen, F.A.; and Jankowski, J.J. "Dimensions of Early Stimulation and Other Differential Effects on Infant Development." *Merrill-Palmer Quarterly* 18 (1972):205-218.

Appendixes

Appendix A-1

Information Sheet

Note: Much emphasis is placed in this book on parents and caregivers sharing information with each other.

In many circumstances, the young child can be cared for more sensitively when caregiving staff know a great deal about the child's family background and current situation. However, much of this kind of personal information will come only after a relationship of trust has been built up between the caregiving staff and the parents. This kind of information should not be obtained on an application form or in an initial interview but rather informally and naturally over a period of time. The following example of an information form for each family in the program contains a minimal amount of information. Each program staff will have to decide what additional information is needed in order to care well for the baby. Medical and health records should of course be developed by health personnel affiliated with the center. Some of the information will need to be updated periodically, and written information should never be allowed to replace frequent informal conversations and exchanges of information between parents and caregivers.

Any information given to the staff about the child or the family must remain confidential. If the staff sees a need to confer with a professional consultant or with professionals in other agencies, the family should be consulted prior to making the referral. Only on rare occasions, when there is substantial evidence of potential damage to the child if there is no immediate outside intervention, should another agency or individual receive information about a family without obtaining the family's permission.

Information Sheet, p. 1

Baby's Name _____ Birthdate _____ Sex _____

Nickname(s) baby responds to _____

Mother's Name _____ Occupation _____

   Place of Employment (Name, Address, Phone Number) _____

_____

   Hours of Employment _____

Home Address _____

Home Phone _____

Father's Name _____ Occupation _____

   Place of Employment (Name, Address, Phone Number) _____

_____

   Hours of Employment _____

Home Address _____

Home Phone _____

Siblings of Baby:

              Name   Age   If not living at home, where?

_____

_____

_____

Others Living in Home (Not Parents or Siblings)

              Name   Age   Relationship to baby

_____

_____

_____

Emergency Information

Place where mother can be reached _____

   Address _____ Phone No. _____

Place where father can be reached _____

   Address _____ Phone No. _____

Person to call if parents cannot be reached _____

   Address _____ Phone No. _____

Baby's Medical Doctor _____ Phone No. _____

If neither parent can be reached, in case of an emergency, I give my permission for members of the nursery staff to secure medical care for my child.

                  Parent's signature _____

169

Information Sheet, p. 2

Feeding

Has your baby had any feeding problems?   Yes _____ No _____

   If yes, what are they? _____

Does your baby have a good appetite and show interest in food?   Yes _____ No _____

What are your baby's favorite foods? _____

What foods does your baby dislike? _____

Have you noticed any allergies or sensitivities to particular foods?   Yes _____ No _____

   If yes, what are they? _____

Is the baby: Breast fed? _____ Bottle fed? _____

Do you give the baby a vitamin/mineral preparation regularly?   Yes _____ No _____

   If yes, which one? _____

What foods is your baby eating now?

   Fruits _____ Juices _____

   Vegetables _____ Meats _____

   Cereals _____ Milk (Formula) _____

Sleeping

Has your child shown any sleeping problems?   Yes _____ No _____

   If yes, what kind? _____

How long does your baby typically sleep at night? _____

What is the baby's sleeping pattern for the day?   A.M. _____

                                                  P.M. _____

Does the baby prefer to sleep on his or her stomach? _____ Back? _____

Do you have any special ways of helping your baby go to sleep?   Yes _____ No _____

   If yes, what are they? _____

Does your baby usually cry when going to sleep?   Yes _____ No _____

   If yes, how long? _____

Does your baby cry when waking up?   Yes _____ No _____

Does your baby sleep in his or her own room?   Yes _____ No _____

Does your baby sleep in his or her own bed?   Yes _____ No _____

   If no, with whom? _____

Interests

What are your baby's favorite toys? _____

What are your baby's favorite activities? _____

_____

Information Sheet, p. 3

Health of Child

How healthy is your baby? _____

Does your baby have any handicaps?   Yes _____ No _____

   If yes, what are they? _____

Has your baby had any serious illnesses?   Yes _____ No _____

   If yes, explain _____

Has your baby had any operations?   Yes _____ No _____

   If so, give dates and describe _____

Does your baby have medicine every day?   Yes _____ No _____

   If yes, what and why? _____

Diseases and Conditions: Has your child had any of the following?

	Yes	No
Whooping Cough	_____	_____
Mumps	_____	_____
Measles (Red)	_____	_____
Measles (German)	_____	_____
Chicken Pox	_____	_____
Pneumonia	_____	_____
High temperature (over 103°)	_____	_____
Allergy, Eczema	_____	_____
Injuries	_____	_____
Neurological	_____	_____
Others	_____	_____

   Is there any other information about your baby—special likes and dislikes or ways you give care—that it would be helpful for caregivers to know in order to take better care of your baby?

HEALTH RECORD*

Immunization Chart

Date Given

DPT   _____
Polio Vaccine   _____
Small Pox   _____
Measles   _____

Visits to Doctor

Date	Reason	Diagnosis	Medication
_____	_____	_____	_____
_____	_____	_____	_____
_____	_____	_____	_____
_____	_____	_____	_____

Illnesses

Symptoms   *Treatment*

_____
*To be kept up-to-date during infant's enrollment.

172

Appendix A-2

DAILY INFORMATION SHEET FOR CAREGIVERS
(filled out by parents)

CORNELL INFANT NURSERY
Department of Human Development and Family Studies
College of Human Ecology
Cornell University

1. When, what, and how much did your baby eat or drink last?
   A. Time _____
   B. Type Food _____
   C. Amount _____

2. A. How long did s/he sleep last night? _____
   B. What time did s/he get up this morning? _____
   C. Did s/he sleep well? _____
   D. If the answer to 2C is no, what seemed to be the problem? (e.g., diarrhea, temperature, etc.) _____
   _____
   _____

   E. What kind of mood is/was s/he in? _____
   F. Did s/he have a bowel movement today? _____

3. Is there any other information that will help us take better care of your baby? _____
   _____
   _____
   _____

173

Appendix A-3

Daily Information Sheet for Parents and Caregivers
(filled out by caregivers)

CORNELL INFANT NURSERY
Department of Human Development and Family Studies
College of Human Ecology
Cornell University

Children's Names

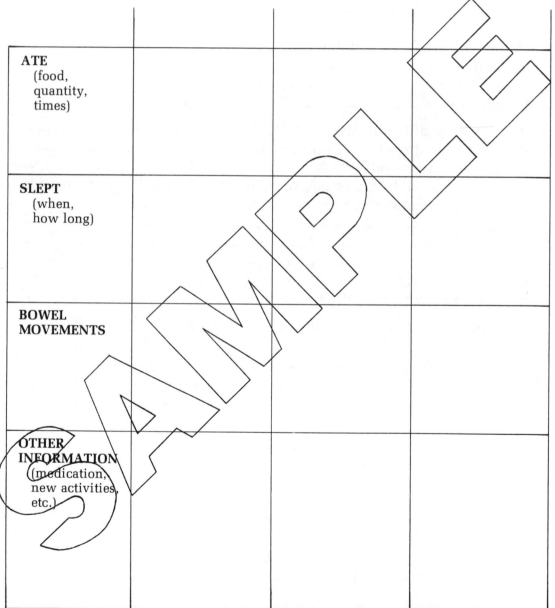

ATE (food, quantity, times)			
SLEPT (when, how long)			
BOWEL MOVEMENTS			
OTHER INFORMATION (medication, new activities, etc.)			

Note: This written information should not be used as a substitute for other communication with the parents.

Appendix B

Outline of Selected Developmental Landmarks During the First Two Years of Life*

CORNELL INFANT NURSERY
Department of Human Development and Family Studies
College of Human Ecology
Cornell University

The outline on pages 176-183 was developed as a teaching aid for students in a course in infant behavior and development. It presents the **approximate** age of typical appearance of a variety of readily observable behavioral characteristics or competencies of infants in the first two years of life. The ages shown should not be taken too seriously, as though they indicated exact points where every baby should show particular behaviors; rather, it should be emphasized that normal babies show considerable variability in the ages at which the indicated landmarks appear.

The developmental landmarks are organized under five general aspects of development: gross motor, manipulative, intellectual, language (comprehension and expression), and social-emotional. These are convenient groupings, but there is much overlap between these areas of development, as indicated by the fact that many behaviors are shown as reflecting the infant's development in two adjacent areas simultaneously.

---

* H. N. Ricciuti, HDFS 374, Spring 1963, Revised January 1973 with Barbara Wolf and Sharon Horner.

These behaviors are approximate ages of "typical" appearance. It should be emphasize that normal children show much variation around the "typical" ages indicated in th outline.

Approximate Age in Months	Gross Motor	Manipulative
1	Head unsteady when held sitting	Both hands fisted; Grasp reflex on contact with object
	Lifts head so 2″ off surface (prone)	Retains rattle briefly before dropping
	Lifts head *and* chest off surface (prone)	Hands mostly open; Reaches toward object (both hands together)
	Symmetrical posture of extremities predominates (supine)	Retains rattle or ring (not reflexive)
	Hands engage in midline	
	Head erect and steady when held sitting; Arms extended, supports weight on hands (prone); Rolls from back to side	Reaches and grasps ring near hand; Pats or fingers feeding bottle; Manipulates or exploits rattle; Drops 1st cube when given 2nd
6	Sits steady with support; Rolls from supine to prone	Grasps objects at midline (predominantly one-arm reach)

Developmental Landmarks

Intellectual	Language Comprehension Expression	Social-Emotional
<div align="center">Attends to sound, activity reduction</div>		Negative and neutral affect differentiable Quiets when picked up
Discriminates sounds; ← → Discriminates visual brightness and complexity; Brief visual following, horizontal		

Visual following, horizontal and
  vertical
	Cooing;
	  repeated
	  vowel sounds
	  (ah, eh, uh)
		Special visual interest in human
		  face;
		Promiscuous smiling and cooing
		  when talked and smiled at

Visual following, circular	Makes 2 different sounds
	  (goo, la, a, ma,
	  mu, uh, eh)
		Anticipatory excitement

Anticipates feeding on sight; Visual inspection of environment; Discrimination of voice quality; ← → Turns head toward sound;	Laughs aloud (Belly laugh) ← →	Shows displeasure at loss of contact with person

Discriminates familiar and unfamiliar faces	Spontaneous
	  social vocalizations ← →
	Vocalizes to
	  toys
		Frolics when played with
		Smiles and vocalizes at mirror
		  image

Glances in direction of disappearing object;
Learns to discriminate simple
  forms
	Vocally indicates pleasure
	  and displeasure ← →
	Makes four different sounds
		Creates social contact (vocalizing,
		  reaching);
		Shows displeasure at loss of toy;
		More pleasurable response to familiar than unfamiliar people

These behaviors are approximate ages of "typical" appearance. It should be emphasiz that normal children show much variation around the "typical" ages indicated in t outline.

Approximate Age in Months	Gross Motor	Manipulative
7		"Rakes" at small edible pellet, can't grasp it; Holds 2 cubes at once; Transfers objects one hand to other
	Supports full weight briefly when hands held	Plays with 2 toys, one in each hand
	Sits alone steadily; Gets self to sitting; Crawls, hands and knees	Picks up edible pellet with "scissors" grasp; Purposefully lets go of cube
	Pulls self to standing	
	Lowers self to sitting; Walks *with* help	
	Stands alone; "Cruises" while standing, holding on to furniture	"Plucks" edible pellet with thumb and forefinger; Places 1 cube in cup
12	Sits down voluntarily; Walks alone	Brings 2 cubes together with hands and examines

Intellectual	Language Comprehension Expression		Social-Emotional
Looks for object which has disappeared			Pats and "plays with" mirror image
Pulls string to secure out of reach toy		2-syllable sounds (dada, baba)	Some negative reaction to stranger's approach; Works persistently to get toy out of reach; Imitates knocking with toy
Uncovers hidden toy			
	Responds to familiar words, (e.g., own name, no-no, mommy, daddy, bye-bye)		
		Uses 1 "word" appropriately	Some self control in response to adult's prohibition
			Protests at separation from mother
Notices discrepancies (shows "surprise")			
		Uses 3 words; Imitates words←	→Playful imitation (pat-a-cake, patting doll); Initiates games with adult
	Obeys simple request ("give me the cup")		
Recovers toy from behind screen			

These behaviors are approximate ages of "typical" appearance. It should be emphasized that normal children show much variation around the "typical" ages indicated in the outline.

Approximate Age in Months	Gross Motor	Manipulative
13	Creeps upstairs	Places 3 cubes in cup
		Releases ball with slight voluntary thrust
		Builds tower of 2 cubes; Spontaneous scribble with crayon
	Walks well; starts and stops with good control; Walks backward with pulltoy; Runs stiffly	Places edible pellet in bottle and dumps out again
		Places round block in formboard ←
		Finger feeds self
	Bends over to pick up toy, returns to standing	
18	Climbs into adult chair; Seats self in small chair	Imitates horizontal crayon stroke; Places 10 cubes in cup
	Throws ball	
		Some management of cup and spoon in feeding self

Intellectual	Language Comprehension Expression	Social-Emotional
Looks at pictures in book briefly with interest		Depressive and anger reactions emerge; also pleasure in "mastery"
		Beginnings of social interaction between infants clearly observed
Attends and pats pictures in book	Uses 4 to 6 clear words	
Shows shoe when asked	Indicates wants ⟵ by gesturing or vocalizing	⟶Spontaneously shows shoe to adult;
⟶	Uses "jargon"	Rolls ball to adult in response to gesture
Hunts for hidden toys in new hiding places		
		May become upset in reaction to adult prohibition
Points to a picture of familiar object when asked (e.g., dog)	Uses 9 to 10 clear words	Enjoys being shown picture book
	Names 1 of 6 test objects	Anger. "Obstinate" behavior frequently observable
Points to one part of doll named by adult (e.g., eye, nose)		

These behaviors are approximate ages of "typical" appearance. It should be emphasize
that normal children show much variation around the "typical" ages indicated in th
outline.

Approximate Age in Months	Gross Motor	Manipulative
19		Places square block in formboard ←
	Walks upstairs, holding rail; Walks downstairs, one hand held	
	Squats and stands up	
	Jumps off step	
		Completes three hole formboard (O△
24	Runs well, seldom falls; Walks up and down stairs alone; Jumps off floor with both feet	Imitates vertical and circular crayon strokes; Helps dress and undress self

Developmental Landmarks, Continued

Intellectual	Language Comprehension Expression		Social-Emotional
Gets toy out of reach by reaching with a stick		Uses words to make wants known	
Follows 2 directions (e.g., put the dolly in the chair)		Uses 12 clear words	
Points to 2 of 4 test pictures named by adult		Combines 2 words (e.g., "daddy gone")	Early signs of "pride," "jealousy;" Pulls adult to show or get help
Points to 5 parts of doll		20 word vo-cabulary	
Begins to recognize forms of same general shape Points to 4 of 6 test objects named by adult; Follows 2 directions with varied objects		Names 3 of 6 test objects; Uses 3 word sentences; Pronouns (I, me, you); "Jargon" discarded	Tries to communicate immediate experiences Well-developed social interaction with peers, especially through use of play materials

Appendix C

Toys For Babies and Toddlers

CORNELL INFANT NURSERY
Department of Human Development and Family Studies
College of Human Ecology
Cornell University

If any common household objects are safe for your baby to have (even if the child decides to see how it tastes), give it to him or her and see what is done with it.

Some ideas for toys that can be made from common objects are:

1. *Shaker bottles*—Put small, colored, edible (in case the bottle is opened accidentally) pieces of dry cereal, for example, inside any clear plastic bottle. Empty, clean, plastic shampoo or dishwashing detergent bottles make great toys for younger and older babies. Be sure the lid is on tightly.

2. *Simple hand puppets*—ones made from socks, for example, are a good way for an adult to talk with a baby. Puppets are a good way for a caregiver to capture children's attention.

3. *Boxes*—all shapes and sizes—for walking or crawling into (refrigerator box), sitting in, stacking, nesting, putting things in and dumping them out. A shoe box with a string attached makes a good pull toy for a toddler.

4. *Sorting toys*—An egg carton or a cupcake tin works well as a place to put objects (large spools, blocks, cereal). If they are unedible, it is important that they are large enough not to be swallowed.

5. *Dress-ups*—Babies enjoy putting on hats, and carrying purses, especially if there is a mirror around so that they can see themselves.

6. *Blocks*—Use milk cartons of different sizes (half-pint, quart, half-gallon). Each block takes two cartons. Cut the tops off and put one bottom inside the other so the bottoms of the cartons make the ends of the block. Put a small edible object inside some blocks so that they will make a noise when shaken. Cover blocks with self-adhesive paper.

7. *Texture Blocks and Scraps*—Cover blocks of wood (approximately 5″ x 3″ x ¾″ and sanded to prevent splinters) with brightly colored fabric of different textures (burlap, corduroy, velvet, quilted material, voile, net).

8. How many things could a baby do with *a cup of dry cereal*? (Yes, one of the first things most babies would do is dump the cereal on the floor!)

9. *Books*—Use books even with very young babies. They like being held, talked to, and looking at the shapes and colors. A relatively "baby-proof" book can be made by cutting large, bright, interesting pictures from a magazine, pasting them on construction paper, covering both sides with clear self-adhesive paper, and putting the pages in a plastic loose-leaf notebook. Old wallpaper books are great for babies to use by themselves.

10. *Hanging Toys*—Many objects around the house (paper cups, spools, aluminum foil pie plates) can be attached to a piece of string or yarn and hung for a very young baby to look at. When babies begin reaching for objects (around four months), suspend objects so that a baby can try to reach while lying in the crib or sitting in an infant seat.

11. *Containers*—Plastic or metal (be sure edges are smooth) containers of all sizes and shapes can be used for stacking, nesting, putting objects, dumping things out of.

12. *Sorting Can*—Cut the plastic lid of a coffee can so that only certain shapes and sizes (blocks, jar lids, spoons, for example) will fit through.

13. *Can of Clothes Pins*—Arrange peg clothes pins around the edge of a can. The baby will enjoy taking them off and putting them in the container. Later the baby can learn to place them on the side of the can.

14. *Hidden Objects*—With the baby watching, put something in a paper bag or box or under a diaper. See if he or she will try to find it.

IF A TOY IS SAFE, IS FUN FOR THE BABY, AND ENCOURAGES THE USE OF THE BABY'S SKILLS, THEN IT'S A GOOD TOY.

Appendix D

Multiple Feeding Table For
Older Infants and Toddlers

CORNELL INFANT NURSERY
Department of Human Development and Family Studies
College of Human Ecology
Cornell University

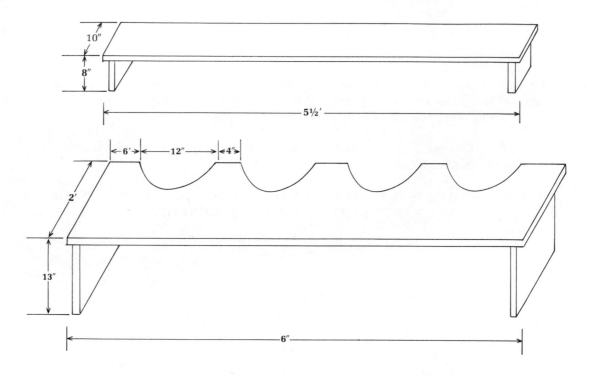

The table is made of ¾" plywood and painted or covered with a washable surface. The bench is placed against a smooth wall to provide back support for the infants, and the table is moved close to the babies so that each one is seated at one of the scalloped openings.

186

Appendix E
Rating Scales for Use With Babies*

CORNELL INFANT NURSERY
Department of Human Development and Family Studies
College of Human Ecology
Cornell University

1. AFFECTIVITY

4–Exceptionally good day—happy, bubbly, smiled and laughed a lot.

2–Very good day—contented, happy, but not as bubbly and excited as 4.

0–Good day—sober, so-so, not irritable but not sunny.

–2–Fair day—cranky, fussed a lot, or just seems sad.

–4–Miserable day—cried a lot, something seems wrong.

2. PERSISTENCE

Persistence is distinct from level of attention in that persistence necessarily involves some problem the child is having in a goal-directed activity. The category includes motor and other problem-solving activities (getting something out of a box, trying to stand up, etc.). Persistence refers to the child's way of coping when on his or her own—that is, before or without the caregiver's intervention.

1–Gives up right away, after first attempt.

2–Gives up after some sustained but minimal effort—minimal attempt to reach goal.

3–Shows sustained goal approach behavior despite some failures.

4–Makes continued efforts despite blockage but does not get upset—much sustained effort, no deterioration.

5–Makes sustained attempts but compromises when failure seems inevitable—pursues less difficult related goal.

6–Makes repeated attempts to reach goal even after failure seems inevitable—continues in spite of distress to point of less effective performance—continues efforts beyond point at which rater feels there ought to be some change in the activity

---

*A report on the developmental use of the rating scales in the Cornell Nursery, including some data, can be obtained by writing to the authors of the book.

3. LEVEL OF ATTENTION

1–Always fleeting attention to activity; minimal involvement; plays only halfheartedly—indicated by child's being easily distracted.

2–Sometimes 1, sometimes 3.

3–Typically intermittent interest in activities; bursts of interest; responds to moderate distractions; child is attentive but may look away occasionally or briefly stop activity for no obvious reason.

4–Sometimes 3, sometimes 5 or 6.

5–Typically deep involvement in activities, absorbed; not easily distracted—for short periods of time (less than one minute).

6–Same as 5 but for longer periods of time (several minutes).

4. SENSITIVITY

This scale is concerned with negative reactions to changes in the environment. Sensitivity refers to a response to something outside the baby (i.e., not hunger, sleepiness, illness).

1–Usually shows little or no negative response even to large changes in the environment (for example, other baby crying nearby, caregiver absent, stranger close and interacting, sudden "assault" by another baby, sudden loud noise, change in routine, other baby taking toy).

2–Occasionally shows some negative response to large change in the environment.

3–Usually shows some negative response to moderate changes in environment (other baby crying in room, stranger present in room, persistent noise, increase in activity level in room).

4–Occasionally shows some negative response to small changes in the environment.

5–Usually shows some negative response even to very small changes in environment (e.g., change in lighting, slight increase in noise or activity level in the room, change in position, light touch, other baby approaching).

If an observable stranger reaction occurs, make a separate rating on this scale by placing an "S" next to the point in the column that describes the reaction. If no such rating is made, we assume either that the caregiver didn't see a reaction or that the reaction was positive.

5. ACTIVITY

1–Engages in few activities, spends a lot of time seemingly doing nothing.

3–Engages in moderate number of different types of activities.

5–Engages in many activities; always is busy.

188

6. QUIETING AND CONSOLABILITY

Use this scale to rate awake time only.

1–Makes no attempt to quiet himself or herself and cannot be socially soothed.

2–Tries unsuccessfully to quiet self and cannot be socially soothed.

3–Does not try to quiet self; sometimes quiets with intensive soothing.

4–Cannot quiet self; sometimes quiets with intensive soothing.

5–Tries but cannot quiet self; requires intensive soothing (rocking, carrying).

6–Typically requires moderate (picked up) to intensive soothing.

7–Occasionally is able to quiet self but usually has to be picked up to be soothed.

8–Typically quiets with minimal (talking at a distance, rocking) to moderate soothing.

9–Typically quiets self or requires only minimal amount of soothing.

7. INITIATION OF EXPLORATION

1–Seldom or never initiates nonsocial play, becomes involved only as a result of another's (usually caregiver's) initiation.

2–Occasionally initiates activities but more characteristically waits to be shown or helped to begin.

3–Typically seeks out or sets up own interactions without another's assistance, but sometimes waits to be helped or shown what to do.

4–Initiates most of interactions with environment on own; does not rely on suggestions of others or help to begin play.

Appendix F

Checklist of Developmental Landmarks

CORNELL INFANT NURSERY
Department of Human Development and Family Studies
College of Human Ecology
Cornell University

	Date First Seen	Dates Seen Consistently (at least 2 times)
Gross Motor		
Lifts head from mattress		
Rolls from side to side		
Lifts head and chest		
Holds head steady when held in sitting position		
Makes swimming motion		
Maintains weight when pulled to standing		
Rolls from stomach to back		
Rolls from back to stomach		
Scoots backward or forward		
Creeps (abdomen on floor)		
Sits alone		
Goes from sitting to crawling		
Goes from crawling to sitting		
Pulls self to standing		
Crawls		
Walks with help		
Stands alone		
Walks alone		
Climbs up and down steps, ladder		
Manipulative		
Bats at object		
Grasps object placed in hand		
Watches or plays with hands or feet		
Reaches for and grasps object at midline or placed nearby		
Transfers object from one hand to other		
Holds own bottle		
Holds two objects		
Feeds self—finger foods		
Feeds self—with spoon		
Uses one hand independently		
Puts object in container		
Picks up object with thumb or forefinger		
Stacks blocks or rings		

	Date First Seen	Dates Seen Consistently (at least 2 times)
Perceptual-Cognitive Visually follows moving object Imitates simple behaviors Recognizes bottle Actively searches for hidden object		
Language Coos and babbles Makes several different sounds Vocalizes in response to caregiver's voice Responds to own name Turns to things or persons when they are named Says word other than mama, dada		
Social Definite social smile Shows interest in other babies Reacts differently to familiar and strange people		

Appendix G

Letter to Parents Regarding Illness

CORNELL INFANT NURSERY
Department of Human Development and Family Studies
College of Human Ecology
Cornell University

Note: This letter is intended as an *example only* for center directors and health personnel. Each center should develop its own policy and procedures and communicate them clearly to parents. Policies will depend on many factors, such as whether or not a sick child can be cared for away from other children.

TO PARENTS:

When is a baby too sick or contagious and therefore should not be brought into the nursery? This is a question which may present itself during your baby's stay at the nursery. In order to protect your baby and the other babies, we have set up some guidelines on illnesses. If at any time the nurse feels that the child is too sick or contagious, he or she will not be allowed into the nursery. So please have a friend or babysitter on call to keep your baby in case you cannot.

KEEP A BABY AT HOME IF HE / SHE HAS:

1. Rectal temperature of over 101° in the morning.
2. Conjunctivitis, which is an eye infection commonly referred to as "pink eye." The eye is generally red with some burning and there is thick yellow drainage being secreted.
3. Bronchitis. This can begin with hoarseness, cough, and a slight elevation in temperature. The cough may be dry and painful, but it gradually becomes productive.
4. Rashes that you cannot identify or that have not been diagnosed by a physician.
5. *Impetigo* of the skin. Shows up as red pimples. These eventually become small vesicles surrounded by a reddened area. When the blister breaks, the surface is raw and weeping. The lesions occur in moist areas of the body such as the creases of the neck, groin and under arm, face, hands, or edge of diaper.
6. Diarrhea (watery or greenish bowel movements that look different and are much more frequent than usual).
7. Vomiting (more than the usual "spitting up").
8. Severe cold with fever, sneezing and nose drainage.
9. If a baby seems really sick without obvious symptoms. In this case, a child may look and act different. There may be unusual paleness, irritability, unusual tiredness, or lack of interest.

192

10. With contagious diseases, a child must be kept at home. Some of these are:
    a) measles (Red or German)
    b) chicken pox
    c) mumps
    d) roseola
11. If a doctor diagnoses an ear or throat infection, for example, and places the baby on an antibiotic, the baby should not be brought in until he/she has had medication for at least 24 hours.

If a baby has a slight fever (less than 101°), a cold, an allergic rash, diaper rash, prickly heat, a loose bowel movement, dietary or medication diarrhea, he or she can be brought to the nursery. We will have a card file of common infections and conditions of babies, their symptoms and treatment, on file in the nursery for use by parents and caregivers.

By helping us to observe good health standards, you will be protecting your baby and the others in the nursery.

Thank you for your cooperation.

Appendix H

Some Guidelines for Caregivers:
Symptoms and Injuries Requiring Special Medical Attention

CORNELL INFANT NURSERY
Department of Human Development and Family Studies
College of Human Ecology
Cornell University

1. Baby *looks* different or *acts* different.
   —Unusual paleness, unusual tiredness, unusual drowsiness, lack of interest, unusual irritability, anxiousness, restless, prostration
2. *Fever*
   —if baby has fever *over 101°*
   —if baby seems more seriously ill or looks sicker even with a temperature of 101° or less
3. *Colds*
   —if more than mild (accompanied by tight cough, wheezing, pallor, etc.)
   —looks sicker, more symptoms (see #1)
4. Hoarseness of voice and difficulty in breathing
5. Sudden decrease in appetite
   —if it continues for several days with additional symptoms
6. *Vomiting* (does not mean spitting up after meals)
   —if baby looks sick, acts different (see #1)
7. *Serious Diarrhea* (watery or greenish bowel movements that look different and are much more frequent than usual)
8. *Blood in bowel movement*—or in vomitus
9. *Inflammation of eye* or injury
10. *Injury to head*
    —if baby is not alert and normally active within 15 minutes
11. *Injury to a limb*
    —shows pain on using it
    —is not inclined to use it normally
12. *Burns*
    —especially if blisters appear
13. *Poisons*
    —reach doctor or poison center immediately
14. *Cuts*
    —if severe
15. *Nosebleed*
    —if it does not stop within 10 minutes
16. *Rashes*
    —almost all

194